Coping with Behavioral Addictions

The Food Addiction Workbook

Information, Assessments, and Tools for Managing Life with a Behavioral Addiction

Ester R.A. Leutenberg and John J. Liptak, EdD

Whole Person Associates

101 West 2nd Street, Suite 203
Duluth, MN 55802-5004

800-247-6789

Books@WholePerson.com
WholePerson.com

The Food Addiction Workbook

Editorial Director: Jack Kosmach
Art Director: Mathew Pawlak
Cover Design: Adam Sippola
Editor: Peg Johnson

Library of Congress Control Number: 2021951010
ISBN:978-1-57025-365-2

From the co-authors, Ester and John,
Our gratitude, thanks, and appreciation
to the following professionals:

—————————— ❧ ○ ❧ ——————————

Editorial Directors – Jack Kosmach and Peg Johnson

Editor and Lifelong Teacher – Eileen Regen, MEd, CIE

Reviewer – Niki Tilicki, MA Ed

Proofreader – Jay Leutenberg, CASA

Art Director – Mathew Pawlak

—————————— ❧ ○ ❧ ——————————

A Special Thank You
to
Whole Person Associates

for their interest in mental health issues.

Free PDF Download Available

To access your free PDF download of the assessment tools
and all of the reproducible activities in this workbook, go to:
https://WholePerson.com/store/TheFoodAddictionWorkbook1010.html

Understanding Behavioral Addictions

There are many types of addictions. The addictions that have been talked about most have been substance abuse addictions. However, behavioral addictions can occur that take the same form as a physical dependence on substances. According to the American Addiction Centers (2019):

> ...it is the compulsive nature of the behavior that is often indicative of a behavioral addiction, or process addiction, in an individual. The compulsion to continually engage in an activity or behavior despite the negative impact on the person's ability to remain mentally and/or physically healthy and functional in the home and community defines behavioral addiction. The person may find the behavior rewarding psychologically or get a "high" while engaged in the activity but may later feel guilt, remorse, or even overwhelmed by the consequences of that continued choice. Unfortunately, as is common for all who struggle with addiction, people living with behavioral addictions are unable to stop engaging in the behavior for any length of time without treatment and intervention.

People are increasingly experiencing non-substance behavioral addictions and their diminished control over the behavior. No longer categorized as impulse disorders, behavioral addictions are now being viewed as true addictions much like substance abuse.

The National Institute of Health (2010) states:

Growing evidence suggests that behavioral addictions resemble substance addictions in many domains, including natural history, phenomenology, tolerance, comorbidity, overlapping genetic contribution, neurobiological mechanisms, and response to treatment.

> The concept of addiction, for years adopted solely to indicate the use of psychotropic substances, is now being applied to describe a heterogeneous group of syndromes known as "behavioral addictions," "no-drug addictions," or "new addictions." Prevalence rates for such conditions, taken as a whole, are amongst the highest registered for mental disorders with social, cultural and economic implications. Individual forms of behavioral addictions are linked by a series of psychopathological features that include: repetitive, persistent and dysfunctional behaviors, loss of control over behavior in spite of the negative repercussions of the latter, compulsion to satisfy the need to implement the behavior, initial well-being produced by the behavior, craving, onset of tolerance, abstinence and, ultimately, a progressive, significant impairment of overall individual functioning.

Grant, et al, 2010

Why Are They Called Behavioral Addictions?

Behavioral addictions constitute any maladaptive pattern of excessive behavior that manifests in physiological, psychological, and cognitive symptoms such as:

- **Continuance:** continuing the behavior despite knowing that this activity is creating or exacerbating physical, psychological, and/or interpersonal problems.
- **Intention effects:** inability to stick to one's routine, as evidenced by exceeding the amount of time devoted to the behavior or consistently going beyond the intended amount.
- **Lack of control:** unsuccessful attempts to reduce the level of the behavior or cease it for a certain period of time.
- **Reduction in activities:** as a direct result of the behavior, social, familial, occupational, and/or recreational activities occur less often or are stopped.
- **Time:** a great deal of time is spent preparing for, engaging in, and recovering from the behavior.
- **Tolerance:** increasing the amount of the behavior in order to feel the desired effect, being it a "buzz" or a sense of accomplishment.
- **Withdrawal:** in the absence of the behavior the person experiences negative effects such as anxiety, irritability, restlessness, and sleep problems.

Addiction to Food

For a long time there has been discussions among professionals that specific kinds of foods may be addictive and that overeating, for example, could be described as a binge disorder. Numerous articles describe the applicability of those DSM-IV substance dependence criteria and other features of addicted behavior to bulimia nervosa, binge eating disorder, obesity, and overeating. While the human body needs food to provide energy and nutrition to perform daily functions, people can feel addicted to food and become dependent on certain types of foods. It is important to note that any food can bring on addictive tendencies.

Some food addiction facts:

- The addictive potential of certain foods, such as those with high levels of carbohydrates or fat, qualifies food addiction much like a substance-use disorder.

- Despite not being recognized as a formal diagnosis in DSM-5, most healthcare professionals still use the term food addiction when referring to someone who displays a food issue of any kind.

- Some foods with high sugar, fat, or starch content are associated with typical food addictions. While these foods are not inherently addictive, their flavor can make them easy to eat compulsively.

- Food addiction is similar to other addictions in that some people can't control themselves around certain foods regardless of how hard they try.

- Despite not wanting to eat, people addicted to food repeatedly eat large amounts of unhealthy foods knowing full well that doing so may cause physical, social, and psychological harm.

Yale Food Addiction Scale

With the development of the Yale Food Addiction Scale (Gearhardt, Corbin, and Brownell, 2009) enough research is being conducted for Food Addiction to be included in the next updated version of the DSM. According to the YFAS, the most common food addiction symptoms as assessed with the YFAS include the following:

1. A persistent desire or unsuccessful efforts to cut down or control eating.
2. Continued eating despite physical or psychological problems and tolerance.
3. Consumption of large amounts.
4. Consumption over a longer period than intended.
5. Spending much time obtaining food, eating, or recovering from a food's effects.
6. Giving up important activities.
7. Withdrawal symptoms when attempting to cut down.

Many parallels exist between new DSM-5 Criteria and overeating: 1) The term craving does not only refer to drug-related substances, but also to other substances like food or non-alcoholic beverages. 2) A failure to fulfill major role obligations at work, school, or home resulting from addiction-like eating. 3) Social and interpersonal problems can clearly be observed in the context of eating behavior. 4) Eating while driving impairs driving performance and increases the risk for crashes. 5) An addiction to eating can greatly damage a person's health and well-being.

The constant preoccupation with eating can be a behavioral addiction that can be treated effectively using a range of cognitive and behavioral therapies.

Signs of a Potential Food Addiction

One can have a food addiction without being totally out of control. An addiction to food is evident when compulsive eating begins to disrupt various aspects of one's life, including relationships, family, friendships, and workplace performance. As the intensity of one's compulsive eating increases, the person is at risk of becoming addicted to food.

Symptoms of a Person with a Food Addiction

The symptoms of food addiction can be physical, emotional, and social.

People with a food addiction may experience:
- The need to eat alone to avoid attention.
- An urge to eat food for emotional release.
- Continued binging or compulsive eating.
- Eating to the point of physical discomfort or pain.
- A preoccupation to obtain and consume food.
- Constant attempts to stop overeating, followed by relapses.
- Negative impact on family life, social interaction, and finances.
- Eating a craved food to the point of feeling excessively stuffed and ill.
- Guilty feelings after eating particular foods, yet eating them again soon after.
- Making excuses about why responding to a food craving is a good idea.
- Loss of control over the quantity, regularity, and location at which eating occurs.
- The need to hide the consumption of unhealthy foods or unhealthy eating habits from others.
- A determination to eat a small amount of craved food and then eating much more than intended.
- Frequent cravings for certain foods, despite feeling full and having just finished a nutritious meal.
- Repeated but unsuccessful attempts to quit eating certain foods, or to set rules for when eating them is allowed, such as cheat meals or on certain days.
- The feeling of being unable to control the consumption of unhealthy foods, despite knowing that this causes physical harm or weight gain.

Those with a mild food addiction may exhibit between four and five of these behaviors, while those with a moderately severe food addiction may exhibit six to seven of these behaviors. People who suffer from a severe food addiction will often exhibit almost all of the above behaviors.

Negative Aspects of a Food Addiction

After compulsively consuming large quantities of food, people addicted to food often experience negative feelings such as these:

- Shame
- Guilt
- Discomfort
- Reduced self-worth

Food addiction can also trigger physical responses such as these:

- Intensive food restriction
- Compulsive exercise
- Self-induced vomiting

Some Food Addiction Facts

An addiction to food is much like any other addiction.

- The idea that a person can be addicted to food is gaining increasing support. This support comes from research, brain imaging, and other studies of the effects of compulsive overeating on pleasure centers of the brain.
- The effects of certain foods on the brain make them difficult for some people to avoid.
- Experiments show that for some people, the same reward and pleasure centers of the brain that are triggered by addictive drugs like alcohol, cocaine, and heroin are also activated by food, especially highly palatable foods. Highly palatable foods are those rich in sugar, fat, and salt.

How Food Addiction Works

An addiction to food is much like an addiction to other substances and works like this:

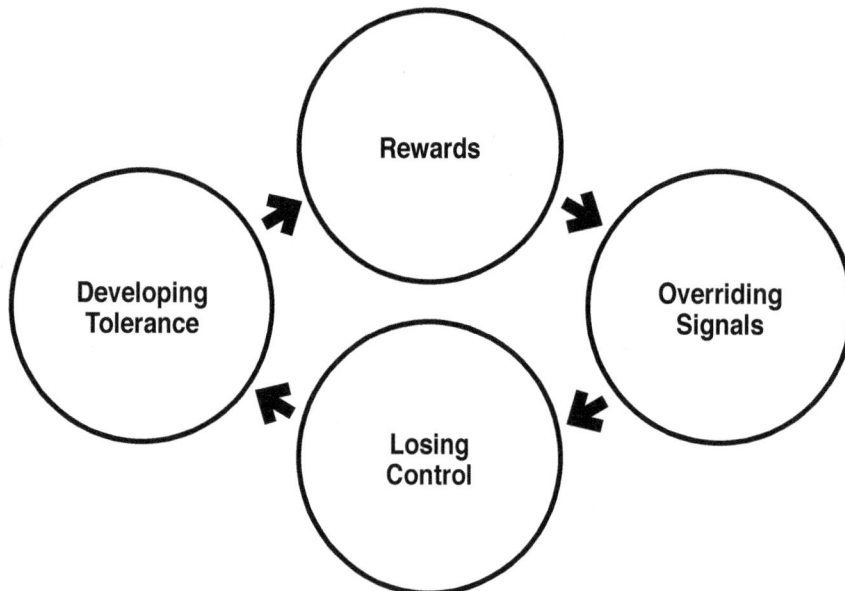

Reward System: This system rewards the brain when people do things that encourage survival-like overeating. Just like addictive drugs, highly palatable foods trigger feel-good brain chemicals such as dopamine. Often, when people experience pleasure from eating certain foods, they quickly feel the need to eat again. The brain is hardwired to seek out behaviors that release dopamine in the reward system.

Signals of Fullness: The reward signals from highly edible foods often override other signals of fullness and satisfaction. People addicted to food keep eating, even when not hungry. Compulsive overeating is a type of behavioral addiction in which people are preoccupied with eating because it triggers intense pleasure.

Losing Control: People with food addictions often lose control over their eating habits. They find themselves spending excessive amounts of time involved with food and overeating, or anticipating the emotional effects of compulsive overeating.

Tolerance: People who show signs of food addiction may develop a kind of tolerance to food. They eat more and more, only to find that food satisfies them less and less.

Using This Workbook

The purpose of *The Food Addiction Workbook* is to provide helping professionals with cognitive and behavioral assessments, tools, and exercises that can be utilized to treat the root psychological causes of a food addiction. It is designed to help people identify and change negative, unhealthy thoughts and behaviors that may have led to a food addiction. The activities contained in this workbook can assist participants to identify their triggers that can lead to an addiction to food, and teach them ways to overcome and manage those triggers.

The Food Addiction Workbook **will help participants to help themselves in these ways:**

- Recognize that they are experiencing an addiction problem.
- Reflect and become aware of the behaviors that were part of, and arose from, the addiction.
- Build self-esteem in positive capabilities outside of eating.
- Understand the triggers for preoccupation with various aspects of eating behavior.
- Develop greater self-acceptance and the ability to change ineffective behaviors.
- Understand recurring patterns that indicate an addiction to food.
- Learn ways to live a new life without the need to obsess about eating food.

The Food Addiction Workbook is a practical tool for teachers, counselors, and helping professionals in their work with people affected by an addiction to food. Depending on the role of the person using this workbook and the specific group's or individual's needs, the modules can be used either individually or as part of an integrated curriculum. The facilitator may choose to administer one of the activities with a group or administer some of the assessments over one or more days as a workshop.

Confidentiality When Completing Activity Handouts

Participants will see the words "NAME CODES" on some of the activities in the modules. Instruct participants that when writing or speaking about anyone, they need to use name codes for people to preserve privacy and anonymity. This will allow participants to explore their feelings without hurting anyone's feelings or fearing gossip, harm, or retribution. For example, a friend named **Megan** who **D**rives **A V**olkswagen might be assigned a name code of **DAV** for a particular exercise. In order to protect others' identities, they will not use people's actual names or initials, just NAME CODE.

The Five Modules

This workbook contains five separate modules of activity-based handouts that will help participants learn more about themselves and about their addiction to food. These modules serve as avenues for self-reflection and group experiences revolving around topics of importance in the lives of the participants in the group.

The activities in this workbook are user-friendly and varied to provide a comprehensive way of analyzing, strengthening, and developing characteristics, skills, and attitudes for overcoming an addiction to food.

The activities in this workbook are reproducible. Minor modifications are permitted to suit participants. Copyright is retained by the authors and must be included on reproduced materials.

Module 1: Dealing With Cravings
> This module helps participants investigate their eating behaviors and cravings. The module explores why people have cravings, ways to distract themselves from these cravings, healthy substitutes for cravings, and the long-term consequences of binge eating.

Module 2: Emotional Eating
> This module helps participants to explore why they turn to food when they are feeling a variety of emotions: understand their eating schedule, identify eating triggers, learn effective ways of coping without eating, and learn how to be more mindful while eating.

Module 3: Consequences of a Food Addiction
> This module helps participants examine the consequences of problem eating behavior, the physical consequences of poor eating habits, their eating behaviors and how they can affect self-esteem, and the ways people who are addicted to food attempt to isolate themselves socially from family and friends.

Module 4: Healthy Routines
> This module helps participants be more mindful of their eating behaviors, rely on exercise to help curb eating behaviors, enhance good sleep behaviors, use physical activity to think less about eating, set goals for effective eating behaviors, and avoid junk food.

Module 5: Coping Strategies
> This module helps participants discover ways to cope with their addiction to food by planning healthy ways of shopping for groceries, exploring how they see themselves when they look in the mirror, and identifying people to whom they compare themselves.

Different Types of Activity Handouts Included in this Workbook

A variety of materials are included in this reproducible workbook:

- **Action Plans** that assist participants in meeting the goals and objectives of treatment.

- **Assessments** that prompt participants to explore their behavior. Often these assessments occur in both pre-test and post-test format to encourage participants to track their progress.

- **Drawing and Doodling** to unleash the power of the right side of the brain.

- **Educational Pages** that provide insights and tips related to the topic.

- **Group Activities** to encourage collaboration among participants and group thinking.

- **Journaling Activities** designed to help participants clarify their thoughts and feelings, thus gaining helpful self-knowledge.

- **Positive Affirmations** that challenge participants to create formidable affirmations to post and to repeat to oneself when impulses begin.

- **Quotation Pages** that offer participants ideas to reflect upon and to see how these ideas apply to their own life.

- **Rewards Pages** to encourage participants to remember to reward themselves as they progress toward their goals.

- **Tables** that require participants to reflect on their lives in the past, understand themselves in the present, and react more effectively in the future.

References

American Addiction Centers (2019). Behavioral Addictions.
https://americanaddictioncenters.org/behavioral-addictions

American Psychiatric Association (2018). Diagnostic and Statistical Manual of Mental Disorders (DSM–5).
https://www.psychiatry.org/psychiatrists/practice/dsm

Gearhardt A.N., Corbin W.R., Brownell K.D. (2009). Preliminary validation of the Yale Food Addiction Scale. Appetite. 52:430–436.

National Institute of Health (2010). Introduction to Behavioral Addictions.
https://www.ncbi.nlm.nih.gov/pmc/articles/PMC3164585

World Health Organization (2018). International Classification of Diseases (ICD) Information Sheet.
https://www.who.int/classifications/icd/factsheet/en/

Table of Contents

(Continued on page xiii)

Table of Contents

(Continued on page xiv)

Table of Contents

Food

Dealing with Cravings

Name _____

Date _____

Food Cravings Assessment
Introduction and Directions

Food cravings can be intense and often irresistible! People who are addicted to food find that they usually crave a specific food or drink. Foods high in sugars and carbohydrates commonly cause cravings, but there are others. Any food can cause a craving and be especially difficult to control. Often the greater the impulse and compulsion to eat or overeat, the more difficult it can be to reduce the addictive behavior.

It is vital to explore the problems that your eating behavior is causing in your life. These problems might include damaged relationships, health problems, risky behavior, and problems in the workplace.

The following assessment contains 20 statements that will help you to explore the intensity of your cravings to eat and overeat. Read each of the statements and decide whether or not the statement describes you. If the statement describes you, circle the YES column next to that item. If the statement does not describe you, circle the NO column next to that item.

In this example, the circled YES indicates that the statement describes the person completing this assessment:

When it comes to eating behaviors:
I crave foods high in sugar. . . . . (YES) . . . . NO

This is not a test. Since there are no right or wrong answers, do not spend too much time thinking about your answers. Be sure to respond to every statement.

BE HONEST!

If you choose, no one else needs to see the results.

(Turn to the next page and begin.)

Cravings Assessment (page 1)

Name _____ Date _____

This will only be accurate if you respond honestly. No one else needs to see this if you choose.

When it comes to eating behaviors:

I crave foods high in sugar. . . . . .YES. . . . . .NO

I crave food when I'm stressed. . . . . .YES. . . . . .NO

I crave specific types of food (salty, carbs, fatty, etc.). . . . . .YES. . . . . .NO

I overeat when I need to feel comforted. . . . . .YES. . . . . .NO

I have cravings that I cannot control. . . . . .YES. . . . . .NO

I crave food even when I'm full. . . . . .YES. . . . . .NO

I have a hard time denying my cravings. . . . . .YES. . . . . .NO

I often eat much more than I intended to eat. . . . . .YES. . . . . .NO

I will eat until my craving is satisfied. . . . . .YES. . . . . .NO

I make up excuses about overeating. . . . . .YES. . . . . .NO

I feel guilty after overeating. . . . . .YES. . . . . .NO

I find it difficult to eat in moderation. . . . . .YES. . . . . .NO

I hide food and eat it when I have a craving. . . . . .YES. . . . . .NO

I have no control when I have a craving. . . . . .YES. . . . . .NO

I eat in secret so others don't know. . . . . .YES. . . . . .NO

I crave food even after I eat a big meal. . . . . .YES. . . . . .NO

I can't ignore the craving even if the food I crave hurts me physically. . . . . .YES. . . . . .NO

I give in to my cravings. . . . . .YES. . . . . .NO

I don't know what triggers my cravings. . . . . .YES. . . . . .NO

I crave food as a way to cope with life. . . . . .YES. . . . . .NO

TOTAL "YES" Answers = _____

Go to the next page for scoring assessment
results, profile interpretation, and individual descriptions

Cravings Assessment (page 2)

Scoring and Profile Interpretations

The assessment you just completed is designed to measure the extent of your cravings for food.

Count the number of YES answers you circled on the Cravings Assessment. Put that total on the line marked TOTAL on the assessment at the bottom of the page. Transfer your total to this space below:

Cravings TOTAL   =   _____

Assessment Profile Interpretation

By circling even one YES answer, you are presently experiencing problems in your life due to food cravings. The more YES answers you circled, the greater the risk you have for experiencing many issues because of your cravings for certain foods.

The HIGHER your score on the Cravings Assessment, the more of an eating addiction you are experiencing.

0 = Low	10 = Moderate	20 = High

Were you honest when completing the assessment? Is your score valid?

_____

_____

What is your reaction to your score?

_____

_____

Do you feel you need to do something about your eating issues?

_____

_____

Food Cravings

Food craving is:
- Sometimes called a selective hunger.
- Different from normal hunger.
- Intense desire for a specific food.
- Desire to eat more despite feeling full.

It's not uncommon to have cravings, even after eating a fulfilling, nutritious meal. What types of things do you crave? In the boxes, identify the foods and drinks that you crave the most. In the spaces next to each box, write when you most often have the craving.

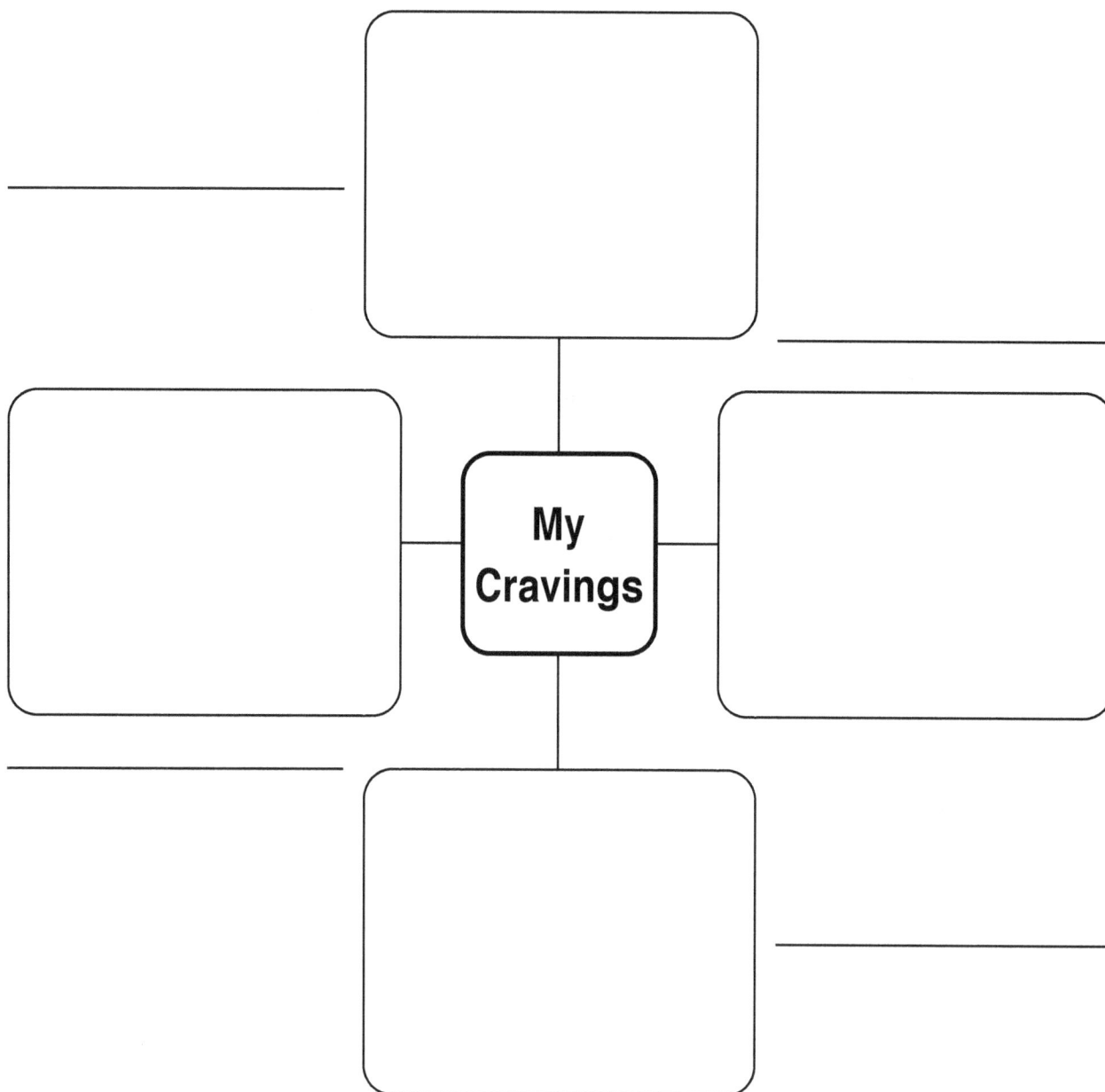

My Cravings

Cravings are very common. While a craving alone doesn't indicate a food addiction, when one often has cravings and ignoring or satisfying them is difficult, it may indicate a problem.

Distract the Craving

People who are addicted to food experience many cravings and urges to indulge. It is important that they learn various methods to distract the craving. This distraction usually involves taking oneself out of the immediate situation mentally and/or physically. Distraction can reduce or totally eliminate your cravings for food and non-alcoholic drinks.

Below, identify some of the ways you have tried to distract yourself and ways you can try to do an even better job with each type of distraction.

Ways to Distract Myself	Have You Tried? Was It Successful?	How Can I Try It and Be Successful?
EXAMPLE: *Drink more water*	*I have tried to drink more water each day, especially when I'm hungry. But I forget!*	*Set a specific amount of water I want to consume each day, and drink a little throughout the day.*
Drink more water		
Eat healthy snacks		
Engage in a hobby		
Socialize without involving food		
Journal		
Exercise		
Reduce everyday stress		
Other		
Other		

What we've learned is that if you can make the right decision in the supermarket aisle, it's a heck of a lot easier to make a good decision when you reach in your cupboard when you're craving a snack at eight o'clock at night.
~ Tom Rath

How does this quote apply to you? _____

_____

_____

Socialize

People with an addiction to food find that cravings occur at any time throughout the day. It is vital not to try and keep your food cravings to yourself. You can call a friend to join you for a walk or go to the gym. You can focus on spending time with friends and family, rather than on your hunger and your cravings.

In the hexagons below, identify the people you can get together with, rather than giving in to your craving. Include how this can help you.

I will
socialize
with...

The Mind-Body Connection

When it comes to eating and managing your food cravings, it is vital to acknowledge the importance of the mind-body connection.

Here are three ways the mind and body connect.

1. Exercise—Rather than giving in to your craving, go to the gym, walk your pet, lift weights, jog, etc.

2. Relaxation—Calm yourself quickly by focusing on your breathing, being mindful of your internal senses and surroundings, or visualizing a calm, quiet place. Remain in that place until the craving diminishes.

3. Meditation—Mindfully stay in the present, and allow thoughts to enter and exit your consciousness without reacting to them.

Draw, doodle, or write the various ways you have used the mind-body connection.

Exercise	Relaxation	Meditation

My Healthy Substitutes

One way to deal with craving is to give in to them with healthy substitutes to take the edge off your hunger. Therefore, if you crave ice cream, you can substitute fat-free or sugar-free ice cream, frozen yogurt, or sorbet. Similarly, if you are craving a candy bar, you could substitute a small piece of dark chocolate or some mini carrots with a small amount of ranch dressing for a dip.

What are some of the foods (including non-alcoholic beverages like soda) that you crave? List them and identify some healthy substitutes you can use.

My Cravings	My Healthy Substitute(s)

I am made for more than a vicious cycle of eating, gaining, stressing...
~ Lysa TerKeurst

Long-Term Consequences

People addicted to food can benefit greatly from becoming aware of their own big picture and remember why they are trying to curb their cravings and restrict their intake of certain foods. Think about the long-term consequences of your food addiction. Some of the long-term consequences might include health problems like diabetes or kidney problems, obesity, yo-yo dieting, reduced energy, less joy, early death, etc.

Visualize the long-term consequences you might face because of indulging in your cravings. Write about, draw, or doodle some long-term visualizations of the consequences of your food addiction.

A Cravings Journal

Journaling can help you become more mindful about your cravings and subsequent eating behavior. By journaling, you will focus your thoughts on the events of the day and record your eating habits, the times of day when you have cravings, and how you feel emotionally during these times. Writing about your eating habits will help you distinguish when you're feeling physically hungry and when you're feeling emotionally hungry.

On the chart below, track your eating habits and emotional feelings for a week.

Days of the Week	Time of Day	Eating Habits	Emotional Feelings
Example: Monday	*6:30 a.m.* *4 p.m.*	*Breakfast – had cookies and ice cream rather than a nutritious cereal.* *Had a whole pizza.*	*I was anxious about my job interview today.* *Relieved it was over. Craved pizza.*
Monday			
Tuesday			
Wednesday			
Thursday			
Friday			
Saturday			
Sunday			

Reproduce this page to journal for additional weeks!

Emotional Hunger

It is important to distinguish the difference between physical hunger and emotional hunger. Physical hunger usually has symptoms like a growling stomach or lightheadedness. Emotional hunger is wanting to eat even though you do not feel physically hungry.

Writing down your emotions towards food will help you identify your triggers and prevent them from happening. For example, you may find you get hungry late at night while watching television and look for a sugary snack. You may want to change your routine to prevent emotional eating by having a healthy snack ready for late-night television watching.

In the spaces below, identify those times you have recently experienced emotional hunger, what you did to manage it, and other ways that may have been more effective.

Emotional Eating Session	What I Did	A Healthier Way I Could Have Handled it
Example: I had a tense day at work and I was still anxious when I was going home.	*I ate food from the refrigerator as soon as I got home and then I wasn't hungry for dinner.*	*I could have taken my dog for a walk immediately when I got home instead.*

I am a better person when I have less on my plate.
~ Elizabeth Gilbert

Do you think Elizabeth Gilbert meant less actual food on her plate? _____

_____

Do you think you need less food, or do you need to eat in a healthy way and reduce the cravings? Explain.

_____

_____

_____

Binge Eating

Binge eating is either eating frequently or all the time until feeling excessively stuffed.

When giving into a craving, people with a food addiction often do not stop eating until their urge is satisfied, whether they are full or not. When this occurs, they realize that they have eaten so much that their stomach feels uncomfortably stuffed.

Identify the foods you crave so much that you binge eat and stuff yourself.

Foods You Binge Eat	When, Where, and/or Why?	The Results	What Can You Do About It?
Example: Ice cream	Every night before I go to sleep I have a pint of ice cream.	I am too full to fall asleep and I am gaining weight.	Have a little sugar-free ice cream for dessert after dinner.

Beverage Craving

A beverage craving occurs when you experience an urge to drink something, despite the fact that you are not thirsty. It is important to pay attention to your cravings and see what or who is causing them, where they occur, and why they occur.

Below, write about your cravings for alcoholic or non-alcoholic beverages.

When	Where	Who	What	Why
EXAMPLE: Evenings	*At home.*	*With my partner.*	*I drink alcoholic beverages.*	*I get frustrated arguing about money and drink.*

What did you learn, or what patterns do you notice?

_____

_____

_____

Things to remember:
- **Beverage cravings are common. Many people can drink alcohol from time to time and are able to manage these cravings.**
- **When beverage cravings happen often, and satisfying or ignoring them becomes difficult, it can be an indicator of a more significant problem.**

Avoid Becoming Too Hungry

The hungrier you get, the higher the chance that you can't fight off an intense craving. It is important to look for solutions before it's too late. Plan your meals ahead and make sure to have a healthy snack by your side if you are prone to craving attacks.

Below are some of the ways to avoid becoming too hungry. For each one, identify how it has been successful or unsuccessful for you, and why.

Ways to Avoid Getting Too Hungry	Successful and Why	Unsuccessful and Why
EXAMPLE: Eat many smaller meals	*This was successful because I was not hungry all the time.*	
EXAMPLE: Eat healthy snacks		*It didn't work. Healthy snacks did not satisfy my craving and it just continued.*
Eat many smaller meals		
Eat healthy snacks		
Set specific meal times		
Eat a lot of protein		
Eat fiber-rich food		
Fill up on water		
Eat meals slowly		
Exercise regularly		
Other		

Say NO

One aspect of a food addiction is that you want certain foods and you crave them because deep down you feel that they will fill a need. When you least expect it, your body is filled with craving and you feel unable to say no. What foods can you not say no to?

Below: write, draw, or doodle up to four foods that you crave.

I crave …

I will attempt to stop craving this food by _____
_____
_____
_____

I crave …

I will attempt to stop craving this food by _____
_____
_____
_____

I crave …

I will attempt to stop craving this food by _____
_____
_____
_____

I crave …

I will attempt to stop craving this food by _____
_____
_____
_____

Let's Hear It for Moderation!

For people addicted to food, it is nearly impossible to eat one bite of chocolate or a single piece of cake. This all-or-nothing approach is common with people who have a food addiction. For them, there is no such thing as moderation. It is important to decide what moderation looks like to you for the foods and drinks you crave.

List your favorite foods and beverages and how much is not enough, just right, and too much.

Not Enough	Moderation/Just Right	Too Much
Example: A pizza – 1 piece	*2 pieces*	*The whole pizza*
Example: 1 glass of wine	*2 glasses of wine*	*3 or more*

Now go back and circle the foods and/or beverages that you always eat and/or drink way too much of.

What can you do about it? _____

_____

_____

_____

© 2022 WHOLE PERSON ASSOCIATES, 101 WEST 2ND STREET, SUITE 203, DULUTH MN 55802 • 800-247-6789 • WHOLEPERSON.COM

Coping with Cravings

People with an addiction to food constantly deal with their cravings.

On the line under each of the ways you have cravings, place an X on the continuum. On the dotted line below each one, write why you rated yourself that way. Be HONEST!

I am obsessed with food.

0 (Not True)   5 (Somewhat True)   10 (TRUE)

I keep overeating even when I know it is not good for me.

0 (Not True)   5 (Somewhat True)   10 (TRUE)

I feel as if food controls me.

0 (Not True)   5 (Somewhat True)   10 (TRUE)

I cannot fight my cravings.

0 (Not True)   5 (Somewhat True)   10 (TRUE)

I eat when anything upsetting happens in my life.

0 (Not True)   5 (Somewhat True)   10 (TRUE)

The higher your score on each of the lines above, the more of a food craving problem you might have in those specific aspects. Areas where you scored low suggest that you are not experiencing many signs of a food addiction in those areas.

Remember that by circling even ONE HIGH response, you are probably at risk for experiencing negative effects in your personal and professional lives.

Coping with Cravings (Page 2)

Now, on the line under each of the ways you might change, place an X on the continuum. Be HONEST!

1. **Will your life change if you overcome your addiction to food?**

   0 (Not Much)   5 (A Little)   10 (A Great Deal)

   ----

2. **Do you want to change your current eating habits?**

   0 (Not Much)   5 (A Little)   10 (A Great Deal)

On the two items above, the higher you scored, the more motivated you are to stop your cravings!

© 2022 WHOLE PERSON ASSOCIATES, 101 WEST 2ND STREET, SUITE 203, DULUTH MN 55802 • 800-247-6789 • WHOLEPERSON.COM

Stress Reduction

Stress is a feeling of emotional or physical tension that comes from any thought or event that makes you feel frustrated, angry, or anxious. Stress is your body's natural reaction to a challenge, a pressure, or an unwanted demand on you. Stress can be a positive thing if it's in short bursts, but too much stress can bring on negative coping mechanisms such as mindless eating.

Try the following quick ways to reduce stress pertaining to the intensity of your cravings.
After you have tried each one below, journal about each one's effectiveness or ineffectiveness.

Swift Calm: While inhaling deeply to the count of 5, give yourself a mantra like "I Am" and on the exhale to a count of 5 say "not hungry anymore." Repeat this as many times as needed to reduce your craving.

_____

_____

_____

_____

The Timer: Set a timer for 15 minutes, then go do something fun until it rings. Know what you are going to do in advance when you begin to feel the craving come on.

_____

_____

_____

_____

Mindfully Eat Something Healthy: Take a piece of fruit or a vegetable and mindfully eat it. Slow your eating down, sense what you are eating, and savor it for as long as you can. Use all your senses to see it, touch it, smell it, and taste it.

_____

_____

_____

_____

Get Out of Autopilot: Bring awareness to what you are doing, thinking, and sensing at the moment of the craving. Get into a comfortable position, notice the thoughts that come up, and let them pass. Stay attuned to who you are and your goals. Do everything possible to enhance your current state of awareness.

_____

_____

_____

_____

Quotes about Food Cravings

On the lines that follow the quotes, describe what one of these quotes mean to you and how it applies to your life. Which of the quotes speaks to you and your current food addiction?

Instead of piling up food in my fridge that says "Come eat me!" I keep enough for only a couple of days. And I rarely have treats around that might tempt me late at night, which is when I usually crave something really fattening. What am I going to do? Drive out at 11 at night just to satisfy a craving? No, that's crazy.
~ Jennifer Love Hewitt

Craving, not having, is the mother of a reckless giving of oneself.
~ Eric Hoffer

I think it's very important to be mindful of your body and actually listen to it. If I'm craving a certain kind of food, I'll have it, but I notice when I'm full. It's kind of like a logical diet. I think when people go on restrictive diets, they put too much stress on themselves, which might make them prone to binging.
~ Samara Weaving

We love salt, fat, and sugar. We're hard-wired to go for those flavors. They trip our dopamine networks, which are our craving networks.
~ Michael Pollan

Which of the quotes speaks most clearly to you and your addiction to food?

_____

_____

_____

_____

_____

_____

_____

_____

_____

_____

Food

Emotional Eating

Name _____

Date _____

Emotional Eating Assessment
Introduction and Directions

People who are addicted to eating often eat when they are experiencing unwanted, negative thoughts. They often overeat, unconsciously aware of the consequences, rather than experiencing and dealing with their emotions in more effective ways.

The Emotional Eating Assessment is designed to help people explore why they might be over-eating. It contains statements that are related to emotional eating. Read each of the statements and decide if the statement is descriptive of your own eating behavior. This is not a comprehensive list, but some of the emotional eating behaviors that one is engaged in excessively can lead to a food addiction.

For each of the items, place a check mark in front of the items that best describe you.

In this example the participant has indicated that both of the first two items apply to them.

    ✔ When I am stressed, I eat more.

    ✔ I eat even when I am not hungry.

    ☐ When I am angry, I eat a lot.

This is not a test. Since there are no right or wrong answers, do not spend too much time thinking about your answers. Be sure to respond to every statement.

BE HONEST!

If you choose, no one else needs to see the results.

(Turn to the next page and begin.)

Emotional Eating Assessment (page 2)

Name _____ Date _____

☐ When I am stressed, I eat more.

☐ I eat even when I am not hungry.

☐ When I am angry, I eat a lot.

☐ I reward myself with food.

☐ When I'm full I eat anyway.

☐ I calm myself by eating.

☐ When I am anxious, I go directly to the kitchen.

☐ Boredom leads me to food.

☐ I tend to eat until I'm stuffed.

☐ I feel powerless around food.

☐ Food makes me feel safe.

☐ I feel as if food is my friend.

☐ Constant eating is a problem over which I have no control.

☐ Loneliness tends to make me eat more.

☐ I often have sudden urges to eat.

☐ I crave specific comfort foods.

☐ I feel an immediate need to satisfy my craving.

☐ I would rather eat than experience unwanted emotions.

☐ I numb myself with food.

Number of items checked = _____

*Go to the next page for scoring assessment
results, profile interpretation, and individual descriptions.*

Emotional Eating Assessment (page 3)

Scoring Directions and Profile Interpretations

The assessment you just completed is designed to measure the extent to which you are engaging in various emotional eating behaviors.

Count the number of items you checked and place that number on the bottom line of the assessment. Transfer that total to this space below:

Number of items checked = _____

Assessment Profile Interpretation

This assessment measures the extent to which you engage in emotional eating. Even one checked item can suggest you are experiencing a food addiction.

The more items you checked on the *Emotional Eating Assessment,* the greater the extent of your addiction to food.

How do you feel about your score?

_____

_____

_____

_____

What steps can you immediately take to reduce your emotional eating?

_____

_____

_____

_____

I Envy the People ...

I envy the people who stop eating when they're stressed.
I'm an emotional eater. I eat my feelings, and, unfortunately, they
aren't fat free. They taste a lot like Ben and Jerry's.
~ Kristen Granata

What does the Kristen Granata quote mean to you?

_____

_____

_____

What do you eat when you are stressed?

_____

_____

_____

What causes you the most stress in life?

_____

_____

_____

How do you feel after you eat your feelings?

_____

_____

_____

What effect does emotional eating have on your life?

_____

_____

_____

How can you deal with stress in a more effective manner?

_____

_____

_____

Why Overeat?

People don't always eat just to satisfy physical hunger. Some people turn to food for comfort, stress relief, or rewards.

Why do you overeat? Write your answer on the lines below.

When I need comfort, I eat rather than _____

_____

When I am stressed, I eat rather than _____

_____

When I reward myself, I eat rather than _____

_____

When people eat emotionally, they tend to reach for carbs, sweets, sugary drinks, and other comforting but unhealthy foods. They may eat ice cream or chocolate when they are feeling sad, order a pizza if they are bored, eat potato chips if they are lonely, or eat fast food after a stressful day at work.

What do you eat? Respond to the questions below.

When I am sad, I eat _____

When I am bored, I eat _____

When I am lonely, I eat _____

When I am stressed, I eat _____

Everyone wants to feel good. They often use emotional eating behaviors to make themselves feel better and to fill emotional needs. There are healthier ways to fulfill emotional needs!

Think hard! What can you do rather than eat? Respond to the questions below.

When I am sad, I can _____

When I am bored, I can _____

When I am lonely, I can _____

When I am stressed, I can _____

My Current Eating Schedule

Irregular eating habits are usually a problem because they result in random eating and overeating. People who are addicted to food tend to eat when they are overly emotional. Eating regularly scheduled meals and regularly scheduled snacks can prevent overeating if you can stick to the schedule.

Complete the schedule below to define your current eating habits. You can adjust the times in the first column to suit your schedule.

Time of Day	What I Usually Eat (Include meals and in-between-meals)
Example: *Pre-6 am* *6:00 am – 9:00 am*	*1 am while watching TV – potato chips and a beer.* *Wake up at 6:30 am – a few cookies before shower.* *7 am breakfast – juice, 2 eggs, and toast.* *8:30 am driving to work – potato chips.*
Pre-6 am **6:00 am – 9:00 am**	
9:00 am – **12: 00 noon**	
Lunch	
1:00 pm – 6:00 pm	
6:00 pm – 9:00 pm	
9:00 pm – Bedtime	

On the next page, you will have the opportunity to create an ideal eating schedule.

An Ideal Eating Schedule

Use these scheduling tips to create an ideal eating schedule that you can follow.

- Schedule three meals and one or two snacks or "mini meals" at specific times of the day.
- Rather than 3 large meals, eat several small meals each day to prevent hunger.
- When you start to feel hungry after a meal, eat a small snack consisting of fruit or vegetables.
- Watch for a signal that tells you it's time for your next meal or healthy snack.

Pre-6 am **6:00 am – 9:00 am**	
9:00 am – **12: 00 noon**	
Lunch	
1:00 pm – 6:00 pm	
6:00 pm – 9:00 pm	
9:00 pm – Bedtime	

Emotional Eating Triggers

People and situations can trigger one's emotional eating. These triggers might include major life events like sickness or daily life hassles like cleaning the house. They can trigger upsetting emotions! These emotions often lead to emotional eating and disrupt one's efforts to overcome a food addiction.

Below, identify some of your triggers, what occurs, what you eat, and how you can avoid this trigger.

My Potential Triggers	What Typically Occurs (Use Name Codes)	What I Eat	How I Can Avoid This Trigger
Example: Relationship Issues	*I get angry with MGW about working so many extra hours, but the money is good.*	*I eat everything in sight that is sweet.*	*I can talk with her about the importance of work-life balance as well as money.*
Relationship Issues			
Work Stress			
Fatigue			
Financial Pressure			
Health Problems			
Family Problems			
Boredom			
Other			
Other			

Types of Foods I Eat

Many people who are addicted to food will indulge and soothe themselves with different types of food when they are experiencing different emotions. One might eat anything sugar-related when angry, order pizza when lonely, or munch a huge bag of chips when anxious.

What foods do you eat to feel better, calm yourself, or soothe yourself when you experience certain emotions? Below, write, draw, or doodle the foods you eat to cope with your feelings.

When I am anxious I eat...	**When I am sad I eat...**
When I am stressed I eat...	**When I am lonely I eat...**
When I am _____ I eat...	**When I am _____ I eat...**

Special Treats

Many people addicted to food often use it as a pick-me-up, a reward, or to celebrate something. When eating is one's primary emotional coping mechanism, one can get stuck in an unhealthy cycle where the first instinct is to reach for an unhealthy treat.

Below, write about or draw the special treats in which you indulge for special occasions.

Foods That Pick Me Up

Foods That Are Special Rewards

Foods I Use to Celebrate

Other than food or drink, what special treats can you give to yourself?_____

_____

_____

Cope Rather Than Eat

Emotional hunger can't be fixed with food. When one eats emotionally, one tends to feel good in the moment, but the feelings that triggered the consumption of food remain. One then feels worse than before because of the unnecessary food just eaten. It will help to identify and have some coping strategies to use when having a craving or eating to satisfy those emotions.

Write about how you have used each of these strategies in the past or would like to use them in the future. If you need more space, write on the reverse side of this worksheet.

Count to ten _____

Listen to music _____

Do something creative _____

Meditate _____

Squeeze a stress ball _____

Mindfully note my surroundings _____

Use support_____

Write my thoughts _____

Play with a pet_____

Take a walk _____

Take deep breaths_____

Describe what I am feeling _____

Monitor my thinking_____

Relax _____

Take a hike or jog _____

Other _____

Mood and Food Journal (page 1)

Before one can break free from the cycle of emotional eating, one first needs to learn how to distinguish between emotional and physical hunger. This is not as easy as it sounds. For people who regularly use food to deal with their feelings, emotional hunger can be powerful and easy to mistake for physical hunger. It is helpful to be able to be aware of when one is physically hungry and when one is emotionally hungry.

A great way to express your emotions (rather than eat) is to write about them in a journal. You can put your feelings into a practical form that will help you to organize, clarify, and express these feelings. Journaling can greatly reduce stress and increase your overall well-being.

Journaling Directions

One of the best ways to identify the patterns behind your emotional eating is to write about it, keeping track with a Mood and Food Journal. Below are some helpful hints.

- Set aside just a few minutes at the end of each day to journal.
- Don't worry about grammar or punctuation. Write without thinking too much.
- Allow it to just come from your stream of consciousness.
- Write it all down in your *Mood and Food Journal.* Describe what happened to upset you or stress you out, what you wanted to eat, why you wanted to eat it, what you ate, how much you ate, how you felt before you ate, what you felt as you were eating, and how you felt afterward.
- Allow time for processing of similar journal entries, ways to manage emotions, and alternatives to giving into cravings.
- Share what you would like to share from your journal with people you trust.

If you make a routine of journaling about your emotions and your emotional eating during the day, you will see emotional-eating patterns emerge. You may find yourself gorging on ice cream when you become angry with your partner. Perhaps you stress eat whenever you have an evaluation at work, or overeat when you are nervous about attending family functions. Once you identify your emotional eating triggers in your journal entries, the next step is to identify healthier ways to manage your feelings.

Page 2 contains a journal page which is available for you to write, doodle, or jot notes about your eating patterns throughout the day. You can make copies of it for the future. It is important to be as detailed as you possibly can be. The third page of this activity allows you to process the entries of your journal.

Mood and Food Journal (page 2)

One of the best ways to identify the patterns behind your emotional eating is to write about it, keeping track with a Mood and Food Journal.

Days of the Week	My Eating Habits Today
Monday	
Tuesday	
Wednesday	
Thursday	
Friday	
Saturday	
Sunday	

Mood and Food Journal (page 3)

It is important to begin to process the results from your *Mood and Food Journal*. By identifying patterns, you can break free from the cycle of emotional eating.

Based on your results from the week of journaling, respond to the questions below:

What did you eat when you were emotionally eating?

_____

_____

What were you eating when you were eating because you were hungry?

_____

_____

What types of foods did you eat when you were eating emotionally?

_____

_____

What types of foods did you eat when you were hungry?

_____

_____

What emotions did you experience before you ate emotionally?

_____

_____

What, most often, prompted these emotions?

_____

_____

How do you, or can you, distinguish between your emotional eating and physical eating?

_____

_____

What did you learn about yourself?

_____

_____

Mindless Eating

When you are eating in response to physical hunger, you're typically more aware of why you are eating. Emotional hunger most often leads to mindless eating. With mindless eating, before you realize it, you've eaten a lot without really paying attention or fully enjoying it.

It is important to become mindful and stay connected to your moment-to-moment emotional experience. This will enable you to manage stress and emotional problems that often trigger unmindful eating behavior.

How to Be Mindful

Mindfulness is the process of concentrating your attention on what is happening to you in the present moment. Mindfulness draws your attention away from your emotions and focuses attention on what you are doing in the present. When you are mindful, you simply quiet your mind, be aware of what is occurring in your body, and observe what is occurring around you.

Next time you are experiencing emotions, try being mindful. What was your mindful situation?

Were you able to quiet your mind? _____

What happened when a thought popped into your head? _____

How did mindfulness help? _____

What was occurring in your body? Did you feel tension in your shoulders? Were you

clenching your teeth, etc.? _____

What emotions did you notice? _____

Did you observe what was going on around you? _____

What did you see, feel, hear, and smell? _____

What did you noticing going on around you? _____

Thoughts that Prompt Emotions

Emotional eating does not occur because one is hungry. Emotional hunger is a craving that starts with one's thoughts that won't get out of one's head. People focus on specific textures, tastes, and smells of the food. If one is constantly experiencing intense emotions such as anxiety, depression, or anger, the person is engaging in a great deal of negative thinking. Rather than eating at a time like this, remember that it is not the situation that is causing you to eat, but the way you are thinking about that situation.

> *Your thinking prompts certain emotions.*
> *You can turn negative thinking into positive emotions.*

Example:

Situation: I fight with my spouse every time we talk about finances.

Negative thoughts: I hate that we are so different when it comes to finances. Why didn't I realize this before we were married?

Emotions: I feel angry and frustrated.

Unhealthy Eating Behavior: I eat a pint or two of chocolate ice cream.

Healthier Response: I will talk with my spouse about my anger and frustration when we are discussing our finances.

Now that you have a formula for successfully reversing your negative thinking rather than eating, try it with one of your negative emotions.

Situation: _____

_____

_____

Negative thoughts: _____

_____

_____

Emotions: _____

_____

_____

Unhealthy Eating Behavior: _____

_____

_____

Healthier Response: _____

_____

_____

Relieving Boredom and Emptiness

People who are addicted to food and eat when they are emotional tend to eat simply to give themselves something to do, to relieve boredom, or as a way to fill an empty void in their life.

When people feel unfulfilled and empty, food can be a way to occupy their mouth and their time.

Complete the following sentence starters to explore your habit of eating when you are bored or feel an empty void.

When I am bored, rather than eat, I could ...

_____

_____

_____

I get bored because ...

_____

_____

_____

Foods I eat when I am bored include ...

_____

_____

_____

When I feel an empty void, rather than eat, I could ...

_____

_____

_____

I feel empty because ...

_____

_____

_____

Foods I eat when I feel empty include ...

_____

_____

_____

Childhood Habits

I still love making hamburgers on the grill. I guess whenever
I eat them childhood memories come up for me.
~ Bobby Flay

Think back to YOUR childhood memories of food and eating. Did your parents reward you for good behavior with ice cream, take you out for junk food, or give you sweets when you were feeling down? Do you remember grilling hamburgers as a kid or baking and eating cookies with your mom? These habits can carry over into your adult life.

Below, describe some of your childhood memories that involve food.

Memories as a Child	Food Habits It Created	Food Habits I Now Have
Example: My parents would take me out for ice cream after every ball game.	*After any of my physical activities I want ice cream!*	*I eat a lot of ice cream.*
Example: My parents ate a lot of vegetables. I didn't like them, but I couldn't have dessert if I didn't eat them.	*I would eat them resentfully to get the dessert.*	*I still don't eat them – but I do eat a lot of desserts!*

From Now On

To stop emotional eating, you have to find other ways to fulfill yourself emotionally. It's not enough to understand the cycle of emotional eating or even to understand your triggers, although that's a huge first step. You need alternatives to food that you can turn to for emotional fulfillment.

If you're sad or lonely, call someone who always makes you feel better, play with a pet, look at beautiful nature or at photos on social media, or call a long-lost friend.

From now on, when I'm **sad** or **lonely**, I will…

If you're anxious, expend your nervous energy by dancing, practicing martial arts or yoga, exercising, squeezing a stress ball, or taking a brisk walk.

From now on, when I'm **anxious,** I will…

If you're exhausted, treat yourself to a hot cup of green tea, take a long bath, read a book, light some scented candles, or get lost in a great movie.

From now on, when I'm **exhausted,** I will…

If you're bored, explore the outdoors, engage in a hobby, play chess against a computer, go to the gym, or join a book club.

From now on, when I'm **bored,** I will…

Quotes about Emotional Eating

On the lines that follow the quotes, describe what one of these quotes mean to you and how it applies to YOUR life. Which of the quotes speak to you about moving on from emotional eating?

The sign of an intelligent people is their ability to control
their emotions by the application of reason.
~ Marya Mannes

The advantage of the emotions is that they lead us astray.
~ Oscar Wilde

All emotions are pure which gather you and lift you up; that emotion is impure which
seizes only one side of your being and so distorts you.
~ Rainer Maria Rilke

Which of the quotes speak to you and help you move forward from emotional eating?

_____

_____

_____

_____

_____

_____

_____

_____

_____

_____

_____

_____

_____

_____

_____

Consequences of a Food Addiction

Name _____

Date _____

Food Addiction Assessment
Introduction and Directions

People who become addicted to food tend to experience consequences that can be physical, psychological, or social, as a result of their eating behavior. It is vital that these consequences are explored so they may then use that information to help limit or eliminate their unwanted eating habits.

The following assessment contains 18 statements related to the consequences you may be experiencing due to your food addiction. This assessment can help you to gauge the extent of your side effects. Read each of the statements and decide whether or not the statement describes you. If the statement describes you, circle the YES next to that item. If the statement does not describe you, circle the NO next to that item.

In the following example, the circled YES indicates that the person completing this assessment believes that the statement describes him or her:

At times …
   I have limited energy. . . . . (YES) . . . . NO

This is not a test. Since there are no right or wrong answers, do not spend too much time thinking about your answers. Be sure to respond to every statement.

BE HONEST!

If you choose, no one else needs to see the results.

(Turn to the next page and begin.)

Consequences of Food Addiction Assessment

Name _____ Date _____

This will only be accurate if you respond honestly. No one else needs to see this if you choose.

At times ...

I have limited energy.	YES..........NO
I have high blood pressure	YES..........NO
I experience digestive problems.	YES..........NO
I have diabetes.	YES..........NO
I am affected by chronic pain or discomfort	YES..........NO
I have heart problems.	YES..........NO

P – TOTAL = _____

At times ...

I feel sad a lot of the time.	YES..........NO
I often feel detached from the world	YES..........NO
I experience emotional ups and downs.	YES..........NO
I have thought about ending it all	YES..........NO
I am unable to enjoy activities I used to like	YES..........NO
I often feel restless.	YES..........NO

E – TOTAL = _____

At times ...

I feel like I'm becoming a recluse	YES..........NO
I'm afraid I'll be teased or gawked at when I socialize.	YES..........NO
I avoid social events.	YES..........NO
I hate the way I look or act	YES..........NO
I have low self-esteem	YES..........NO
I avoid social interactions	YES..........NO

S – TOTAL = _____

*Go to the next page for scoring assessment
results, profile interpretation, and individual descriptions.*

Consequences of Food Addiction Assessment

Scoring and Profile Interpretations

The assessment you just completed is designed to measure the consequences you are experiencing due to your eating behaviors.

In each of the sections on the previous page, count the scores you circled. Put that number on the line marked TOTAL at the end of each section. Transfer your total to the space below, and place an X on the line representing your score:

P=Physical = _____ (Consequences related to your physical body and health).

---
0 = Low   3 = Moderate   6 = High

E=Emotional = _____ (Consequences related to your emotions).

---
0 = Low   3 = Moderate   6 = High

S=Social = _____ (Consequences related to your desire to engage in social interactions).

---
0 = Low   3 = Moderate   6 = High

Remember that even one circled item on a scale can suggest you are affected by your current eating behavior.

The HIGHER your score on the Consequences of Food Addiction Assessment, the greater the chance that your eating behavior and food addiction is affecting your life and well-being.

Re-Engaging

A food addiction can lead to several physical, emotional, and social consequences including digestive issues, heart disease, obesity, low self-esteem, and isolation. A food addict will often re-engage in these destructive behaviors, even amidst undesired consequences, due to the need for induced feelings of pleasure.

Below, identify the foods you tend to crave and/or overeat, the consequences of this eating behavior, and how you can break the eating cycle.

Foods I Crave and Overeat	The Undesired Consequences	What I Could Eat or Do Instead of Eating
Example: Pizza	I am becoming obese. My clothes don't fit.	I can order one piece of pizza and take a walk after I eat it.

The cakes and pies and casseroles beckoned like gastronomic sirens,
and there was no one to lash me to the mast.
~ Chris Fabry

Which foods beckon to you like gastronomic sirens? _____

_____

_____

Physical Consequences (page 1)

People addicted to food often experience many physical reactions to their eating habits. This food issue often results in negative physical consequences to the body as an excess of food is consumed. Below are some physical effects that may be experienced.

With each possible physical consequence listed below, place a check mark in front of the ones that affect you, and describe how your eating habits affect your body physically.

☐ **Chronic fatigue** _____
_____
_____

☐ **Diabetes** _____
_____
_____

☐ **Digestive Problems** _____
_____
_____

☐ **Headaches** _____
_____
_____

☐ **Heart disease** _____
_____
_____

☐ **Lethargy** _____
_____
_____

☐ **Malnutrition** _____
_____
_____

☐ **Obesity** _____
_____
_____

☐ **Pain** _____
_____
_____

☐ **Reduced sex drive** _____
_____
_____

☐ **Sleep problems** _____
_____
_____

☐ **Others** _____
_____
_____

(Continued on the next page)

Physical Consequences (page 2)

People addicted to food often experience many physical reactions because of their eating habits. This food issue often results in many negative physical consequences on the body as an excess of food is consumed.

Below are some physical issues that some people experience. Place a check in front of those that affect you, and describe how your eating habits affect your body physically.

☐ **Arthritis** _____

_____

_____

☐ **Stroke** _____

_____

_____

☐ **Kidney Disease** _____

_____

_____

☐ **Osteoporosis** _____

_____

_____

☐ **Unhealthy Weight Gain** _____

_____

_____

☐ **Headaches** _____

_____

_____

☐ **Malnutrition** _____

_____

_____

☐ **High Blood Pressure** _____

_____

_____

☐ **Others** _____

_____

_____

Fixing Low Self-Esteem

People who are addicted to food often have low self-esteem as a result of their eating behavior or they overeat because of their low self-esteem. They often forget all of the positive things about themselves. The more they eat, the less they like themselves. People with high self-esteem are able to recognize and focus on the things they like about themselves rather than focusing on their deficiencies.

Below, identify some of the things (eating-related or not) that you like about yourself.

Examples: **I like that I** *sometimes try to eat healthy.* **I like that I** *have an outgoing personality.* **I like that I** *help animals while volunteering at the animal shelter.*

I like that I

I like that I

I like that I

I like that I

I like that I

I like that I

I like that I

You're always with yourself, so you might as well enjoy the company.
~ Diane Von Furstenberg

Isolating Myself

Having an addiction to food can be frustrating and often embarrassing. Many people who are addicted to food will attempt to isolate themselves to avoid other people.

In each of the circles below, identify a way that you isolate yourself from other people in your life. Write how and when you do it, and from whom. (Use name codes.)

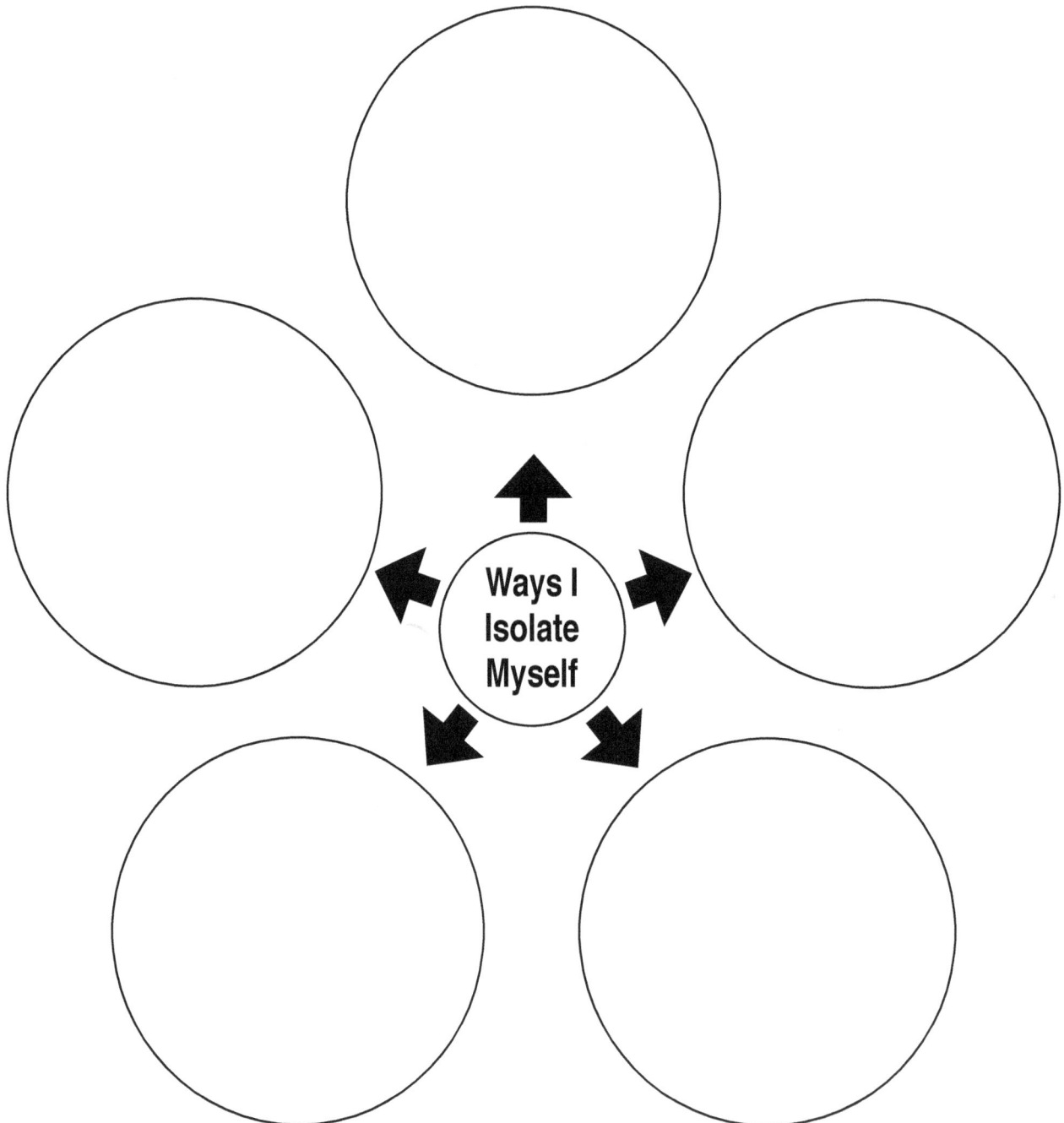

Ways I Isolate Myself

What Happens Following a Binge?

Many people who are addicted feel severe emotional distress following an eating binge. They tend to feel ashamed, guilty, and/or disgusted. This often leads to eating more to try and feel better.

Explore the last several binge-eating sessions in which you engaged, and describe some of the emotions associated with your binge eating.

Binge-Eating Session	Describe it	How Did You Feel?
Example: Thursday night	Fought with my roommate about the rent – ate a gallon of chocolate ice cream.	I felt stupid and angry with myself… there has to be a better way to deal with my feelings.

Tips for Avoiding Binge Eating:
- Stick to a regular eating pattern.
- Stay hydrated by drinking water.
- Eat as slowly and as mindfully as possible.
- Make healthy life changes rather than trying the latest "fad" diet.
- Avoid skipping meals. When you skip meals, you put yourself at risk for overeating later.
- Clean out your kitchen and get rid of binge-worthy food items like potato chips, ice cream, soda, etc.

Other Consequences

The effects of a food addiction can prove intense and plague you for years.

Below, identify the consequences you feel, how you feel, and describe how these consequences affect you.

Consequences	How I Feel	How I Am Being Affected
Example: Hopelessness	*I feel like I will never live a normal life.*	*I stay in the house most of the day, and I only go out for food.*
Hopelessness		
Powerlessness		
Isolation		
Self-Loathing		
Guilty		
Self-Injurious Behavior		
Suicidal Thoughts		
Suicide Attempts		

A State of Hopelessness

People who are addicted to food often feel a state of hopelessness. They attempt to break free of the food addiction cycle but are unable to do so, which makes them feel hopeless. They try to quit, and when they can't, they often just give up.

Below, doodle or draw a picture of what you think you will look like in ten years if you continue eating the way you are now.

If you do not want to look like the picture you drew, you can ...
- **Join a gym and start exercising.**
- **Get enough sleep.**
- **Maintain a food journal of all that you eat.**
- **Understand your food triggers.**
- **Rely on your support network.**

The Bond between Food and Me

Read the following quote and then respond to the questions that follow. Be honest with yourself!

> The bond between food and me is like other relationships in my life: complicated, evolving, demanding, and in need of constant work. But together we've come so far, moving from my childhood obligation to clean my plate, to a mindless need to fill up, to a truly nourishing and pleasurable exchange. That's the real reward.
> **~ Ashley Graham**

How is the food in your life like a relationship?

_____

_____

_____

Why is your relationship with food so complicated?

_____

_____

_____

How does your relationship with food need constant work?

_____

_____

_____

What are you doing to work on your relationship with food?

_____

_____

_____

What childhood messages did you receive about food?

_____

_____

_____

How is your relationship with food becoming more of a pleasurable exchange?

_____

_____

_____

Decreased Performance

Do you regularly experience a decreased performance at work, a volunteer assignment, a chore at home, with your relationships, or anywhere else, due to your eating behavior? Many people who are addicted to food often do.

Write about, doodle, or draw the ways your performance may be decreasing in these areas of your life.

At My Work / Volunteer / School	At My Home with Family

With My Friends	Other_____

My Food Addiction

Aside from the weight issue, people with a food addiction are at risk for social isolation, eating disorders like bulimia and anorexia, problems at work, relationship issues, health risks, and much more.

What types of foods keep you addicted?

Be honest! No one needs to see this page if you choose not to show it to anyone.

Type of Foods	How Much and How Often I Eat or Drink It	The Consequences I Have Noticed
Sugary Sweets		
Sugary Drinks		
Salty Food		
Carbs		
Comfort Food		
Fast Food		
Unhealthy Snacks		
Other		

How can you decrease your dependence on the foods you are addicted to?

_____

_____

_____

Isolation

Do you ever isolate yourself from others because of your eating habits, your weight, or your addiction to certain foods?

On each item below, circle whether the statements are true or false for you, and explain why you believe that.

REGARDING MY EATING BEHAVIOR

I want to hide my food problem from family members. . . . . .TRUE   **FALSE**

Why? _____

I want to hide my food problem from friends. . . . . .TRUE   **FALSE**

Why? _____

I am worried that others will judge me. . . . . .TRUE   **FALSE**

Why? _____

I feel ashamed of my eating behavior. . . . . .TRUE   **FALSE**

Why? _____

I feel lonely. . . . . .TRUE   **FALSE**

Why? _____

I miss regular social contact with others. . . . . .TRUE   **FALSE**

Why? _____

I think that others do not want to be around me. . . . . .TRUE   **FALSE**

Why? _____

Who are some trusted people with whom you can talk about your eating habits? (Use name codes)

_____

_____

_____

_____

Enjoyment? Lack of It?

People experiencing an addiction to food often find themselves no longer able to enjoy certain hobbies or activities. Their food addiction gets in the way! For example, when you go to the pool you may not be allowed to bring food, so you don't go.

Below, identify some of the hobbies and activities you once enjoyed, and why you no longer engage in them.

Hobbies and Activities I Once Loved	Why I No Longer Engage

No hidden talents, but I have a lot of hobbies. Acrylic painting — I got a whole set, and I light candles at night and sit there and paint and look out on Lake Michigan.
~ **Christen Press**

Avoidance

Avoidance = The action of keeping away from or not doing something.

Do you find yourself avoiding social interactions, relationships, and/or functions because certain foods are not available, or because you do not want to embarrass yourself by eating as much as you really want? It would be helpful for you to determine why you are avoiding them, what it is about your eating behavior that makes you want to avoid certain things or people, and how you can find ways to reengage with people and things you love.

Below, explore some of the reasons you avoid people and situations.

People, Social Functions, and Events I Avoid	Why I Avoid Them	How I Can Go and Then Get Help
Example: I hate to go to formal events like weddings.	*My clothes don't fit well. I've gained weight and I can't afford to keep buying new clothes.*	*I can buy something that fits at a thrift store and go. I will talk with M.J.G. to get help with my food habits.*

That is the one single word that the food industry hates: 'addiction.'
They much prefer words like 'craveability' and 'allure.'
~ Michael Moss

Jeopardizing Finances

People with a food addiction often find that they spend an inordinate amount of money on unhealthy food and drinks. They usually don't realize the amount of money they are spending until they really explore the actual amount of money going out for food.

In the hexagons below, write how much money you spend for each category every WEEK.

Be honest! No one needs to see this if you choose.

Chips and Other Salty Snacks

$_____

Other

$_____

Cookies, Candy, and Other Sweets

$_____

How Much I Spend

Comfort Food

$_____

Other Binge Eating Foods

$_____

Fast Food

$_____

Quotes about Food Addiction Effects

On the lines that follow the four quotes, describe which quote(s) speak to you and your food addiction.

If I have one addiction in life, it's probably food.
~ Liam Hemsworth

I love apple sauce. I have an addiction – I don't know what it is, but I just love the texture of it. It reminds me of baby food. Not that I like to eat baby food.
~ Normani Kordei

I always think I am one of the millions and millions of people that struggles with an addiction to food. I don't know how to relax, that's my problem.
~ Carnie Wilson

I have a simple mantra: eat right and work out; you'll never have a weight issue. I never starve or binge.
~ Malaika Arora Khan

Which quote especially speaks to you about your food addiction? Why?

_____

_____

_____

_____

_____

_____

_____

_____

_____

_____

_____

Food

Healthy Routines

Name _____

Date _____

Healthy Routines Assessment
Introduction and Directions

People addicted to food need to eat healthy meals AND exercise. Through this combination, you will be able to slowly and consistently restructure your relationship with food. It should be noted that if you have a serious eating problem, you should immediately consult a medical professional.

The Healthy Routines Assessment contains 20 statements related to healthy eating habits and exercise. It can help you gauge how you are doing. Read each of the statements and decide whether or not the statement describes you. If the statement describes you, circle the number in the TRUE column next to that item. If the statement does not describe you, circle the number in the NOT TRUE column next to that item.

In the following example, the circled 2 indicates that the person completing this assessment believes that the statement is true for them:

	TRUE	NOT TRUE
When it comes to nutrition...		
I eat three balanced meals each day.	(2)	1

This is not a test. Since there are no right or wrong answers, do not spend too much time thinking about your answers. Be sure to respond to every statement.

BE HONEST!

If you choose, no one else needs to see the results.

(Turn to the next page and begin.)

Healthy Routines Assessment

Name _____ Date _____

**This will only be accurate if you respond honestly.
No one else needs to see this if you choose to keep it private.**

	TRUE	NOT TRUE

When it comes to eating ...

I eat three balanced meals each day 2 1

I eat lots of fresh fruits and vegetables 2 1

I have irregular and inconsistent eating habits 1 2

I skip meals and then eat foods I crave 1 2

I often give in to my cravings 1 2

I eat food that contains large amounts of sugar 1 2

I plan my meals ahead of time. 2 1

I eat a lot of fast foods. 1 2

I often eat too much food at meals 1 2

I refuse to give up unhealthy eating 2 1

Eating TOTAL = _____

	TRUE	NOT TRUE

When it comes to exercise ...

I don't exercise if I don't feel like it 1 2

I exercise to keep unnecessary weight off 2 1

I try to stay physically active 2 1

I do not have time to exercise 1 2

I have a long-term exercise plan I stick to 2 1

I set aside a regular time for exercising. 2 1

I keep myself physically fit 2 1

I hate how I look and yet I do nothing about it. 1 2

Taking care of my body is important to me 2 1

I set unrealistic exercise goals and then don't do them. .1 2

Exercise TOTAL = _____

*Go to the next page for scoring assessment results,
profile interpretation, and assessment description.*

Healthy Routines Assessment

Descriptions and Profile Interpretations

The assessment you just completed is designed to measure your eating and exercise habits. For each of the items on the previous page, add up the points of the scores you circled. Put that total on the line marked TOTAL at the end of the sections. Transfer your total to the space below:

Eating TOTAL　　=　　_____

Exercise TOTAL　　=　　_____

Assessment Profile Interpretation

By circling even ONE Number 1 answer, you are at risk for developing or maintaining your food addiction. The more "1" answers you circled, the greater your risk of having a problem with food.

Healthy Routines Total

This assessment measures the impact of excessive eating on your life.

Remember that even one item circled can suggest you are experiencing a problem in your life due to your relationship with food. The LOWER your score on the Healthy Routines Assessment, the more of an issue you probably have with food. Place on X on the scale below closest to each of your scores.

Eating (The quality of your eating habits)

10 = Low　　　　　15 = Moderate　　　　　20 = High

Exercise (The amount of time and effort you spend exercising)

10 = Low　　　　　15 = Moderate　　　　　20 = High

Eating Mindfully

Whenever possible, try to focus on mindful eating. Many people rush through meals or eat in their cars, often not being able to remember what they ate. If you have an unhealthy relationship with food, it is time to slow down and begin to give yourself time for relaxed eating. Start by paying attention to the food you eat. Mindless eating can lead to overeating, not eating enough, eating too fast, and not being concerned about healthy foods.

The next time you eat, try being more mindful using these techniques:

Do not attempt to engage in other activities when you eat. This means sitting at the table when you eat and focusing on what you're eating instead of watching television, working on the computer, or multi-tasking in any way. What can you eliminate while you are eating?

_____

_____

_____

Avoid any distractions. How are you usually distracted when eating?

_____

_____

_____

Notice the sensation and taste of the food. How did the food look? Smell?

_____

_____

_____

Eat slowly. Put your fork down between bites! This will make food more satisfying to you and make you less likely to crave additional snacks. How did that feel?

_____

_____

_____

Pay attention to every bite. Chew. How did every bite taste?

_____

_____

_____

My Addictive Foods (Page 1)

Food is not meant to be addictive, but for many people it is! Research suggests that sugar stimulates the brain's reward centers exactly like other addictive drugs. It also suggests that high-sugar and high-fat foods work just like heroin, opium, or morphine on the brain. It is vital to think about what foods have an addictive potential for you.

Respond to the following sentence starters to explore your addictive foods.

The foods I crave include:

_____

_____

The foods I think about when I'm not physically hungry are:

_____

_____

The foods I want to eat more of, even when I'm full include:

_____

_____

The foods I typically deprive myself of, but feel unable to control myself around later, include:

_____

_____

The foods that have emotional associations for me include:

_____

_____

The foods I remember most fondly from childhood include:

_____

_____

(Continued on the next page)

My Addictive Foods (Page 2)

Respond to the following questions to explore your addictive foods.

The foods that seem to have the power to make me feel better include:

_____

_____

_____

The foods that I tend to binge eat include:

_____

_____

_____

The foods I eat, and later feel guilty about eating, include:

_____

_____

_____

The foods that I eat when I'm lonely include:

_____

_____

_____

The foods that I eat when I am anxious include:

_____

_____

_____

The foods that I eat when I eat fast food are:

_____

_____

_____

Consider driving or walking past the fast food restaurants!

Exercise Inventory

Physical activity and exercise are two of the most effective ways to lessen effects of your food cravings, lessen any stress you are experiencing, and release stuck emotions.

In order to maximize the benefits of regular activity and exercise respond below. Place a check mark in front of the types of exercise you do at least once a week. On the lines below them, describe when and how often you engage in each.

☐ Outdoors around the house: gardening, digging, cutting grass, pulling weeds, etc.

_____

_____

_____

☐ Outdoors: walking, hiking, jogging, running, etc.

_____

_____

_____

☐ Water: aerobics, swimming laps, diving, etc.

_____

_____

_____

☐ Bicycling, skateboarding, rollerblading, jumping rope, etc.

_____

_____

_____

☐ Dancing: ballroom, aerobic, hip hop, lyrical, free style, tap, jazz, etc.

_____

_____

_____

☐ Team sports: tennis, soccer, hockey, basketball. etc.

_____

_____

_____

☐ Gym: exercise on machines, pool, classes, etc.

_____

_____

_____

☐ Other:

_____

_____

_____

Physical Activity Log

Exercise improves your chance of living a healthy life and it relieves symptoms of depression and anxiety. It is helpful to track the physical activity in which you engage during the week.

Physical Activity	How Much Time Per Week?	How Does It Make You Feel?	If You Don't Engage, Why Not?
Exercise			
Ride a bicycle			
Walk, jog, or walk a pet			
Play sports			
Join a gym			
Engage in aerobic activities			
Lift weights			
Practice yoga, tai chi, etc.			
Aerobics or dance classes			
Swim or aquatic exercise			
Work around the house			
Take stairs			
Stretch			
Calisthenics			
Other			
Other			

Go back to the list and put a check by the activities you are willing to do more regularly.

Setting Goals

A GOAL is the result or achievement toward which effort is directed.

It is important for you to set goals for your food habits.

In the sections that follow, write your long-term goal (six months to a year into the future) at the top and three short-term goals (one to three months) to achieve your long-term goals.

Example:

NOW you try!

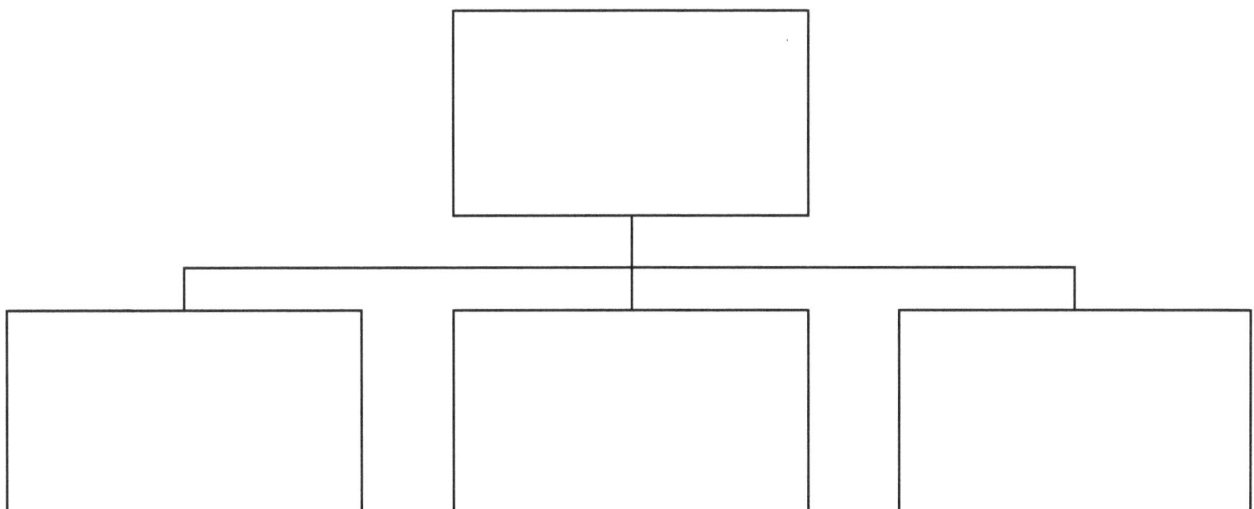

Replacing Process Foods with Proteins

One way to begin your journey to an addiction-free approach to food is by eliminating highly processed foods (which are often frozen, canned, or dried, as well as hot dogs, cereal) and any other foods that trigger you to overeat. You can replace these addictive foods with nourishing alternatives such as good quality protein (almonds, chicken breast, cottage cheese, eggs, fish, Greek yogurt, lean beef, milk, oats, peanut butter, etc.).

In the circles below, list the foods you want to eliminate. Next to them, provide a great substitute protein food.

Foods I Want to Eliminate

Withdrawal

It is vital that you allow yourself plenty of time to withdraw from addictive foods. Eliminating sugar and processed foods can be uncomfortable for several days before the physical cravings subside. During this time, you can expect to be irritable, and experience other symptoms of withdrawal.

How have you felt when you tried to withdraw from your addictive foods?

A Time I Tried to Withdraw from Addictive Foods	How I Felt and Acted	The End Result	What Can I Do Differently
Example: I tried to substitute vegetable snacks for candy snacks.	I was really agitated.	Everyone was mad at me because I was nasty.	Warn people in my life ahead of time!

Beware the hobby that eats.
~ Benjamin Franklin

Sleep to Reduce Stress

It is best to have eight hours of sleep at night, and to plan downtime for yourself during the day. Giving yourself time to de-stress is key to your success. Stress fuels food addiction, and so will lack of sleep. When you are tired, you are more likely to reach for sugar and junk food that gives you a temporary boost of energy. This can feed the cycle of a food addiction.

On the line under each of the sleep routines listed below, place an X on the continuum of how much you relate to the statement. On the dashed line below each one, write why you rated yourself that way.

BE HONEST!

I have a wind-down routine at night.

_____
0 (Not Like Me)　　　　　　5 (Somewhat Like Me)　　　　　　10 (Much Like Me)

I turn off all televisions and computers one hour before bedtime.

_____
0 (Not Like Me)　　　　　　5 (Somewhat Like Me)　　　　　　10 (Much Like Me)

I sleep in a quiet, dark room, without a computer or phone.

_____
0 (Not Like Me)　　　　　　5 (Somewhat Like Me)　　　　　　10 (Much Like Me)

I reduce caffeine consumption before bedtime.

_____
0 (Not Like Me)　　　　　　5 (Somewhat Like Me)　　　　　　10 (Much Like Me)

I avoid physical activity before bedtime.

_____
0 (Not Like Me)　　　　　　5 (Somewhat Like Me)　　　　　　10 (Much Like Me)

I read or listen to soothing music before bedtime.

_____
0 (Not Like Me)　　　　　　5 (Somewhat Like Me)　　　　　　10 (Much Like Me)

The HIGHER (Much Like Me) your score on each of the statements, the better your sleep routine tends to be. Areas where you scored lower (Not Like Me) suggest that you need to revamp your sleep routine to help break the food addiction cycle.

Junk Food

Foods commonly considered junk foods include salted snack foods, gum, cake, candy, sweet desserts, fried fast food, sugary carbonated beverages, and many processed meats and cheeses. Some hamburgers, pizza, and tacos are also considered junk foods because of their ingredients. Simply put, junk foods are not good for you, and sadly, because of their good taste, they are addicting.

Write about, draw, or doodle four of the junk foods that you eat the most and know that you should eliminate them from your diet. Then describe how you will eliminate it from your diet.

Junk Food _____

How I Will Eliminate It:

Junk Food _____

How I Will Eliminate It:

Junk Food _____

How I Will Eliminate It:

Junk Food _____

How I Will Eliminate It:

Wellness Quote

Read the following quote and respond to the questions that follow it.

If you want to become physically stronger, you'll need healthy habits—
like going to the gym. You'll also have to give up unhealthy habits—
like eating junk food. Building mental strength requires healthy habits—
like practicing gratitude — while also giving up unhealthy behavior,
like giving up after the first failure.
~ Amy Morin

What does the above quotation mean to you?

_____

_____

_____

What healthy habits do you want to adopt?

_____

_____

_____

What unhealthy habits do you want to give up?

_____

_____

_____

What unhealthy habits do you know you should give up?

_____

_____

_____

What does mental strength mean to you?

_____

_____

_____

What are ten things or people you are most grateful for that would be even better if you didn't have a food addiction?

_____

_____

_____

Balance

To help overcome your addiction to food, it is important to eat three balanced meals each day and drink water throughout the day. It's important to eat breakfast, lunch, and dinner with balanced portions of good quality carbohydrates, proteins, and fats.

***For one day, journal about everything you eat throughout the day.* BE HONEST!**

Day and Date:_____

Food During the Day	What I Ate	What I Should Have Eaten
Breakfast	*Crunchy cereal, coffee, and a cookie.*	*A couple of eggs, bacon, and juice.*
Breakfast		
Lunch		
Dinner		
Healthy Snacks		
Unhealthy Snacks		

Are you eating balanced meals each day? Here are some eating tips.
- **Never skip meals. Eat every 4-5 hours throughout the day.**
- **Eat on time! This will help to avoid blood sugar fluctuations and keep you from getting hungry.**
- **Eliminate snacking unless you eat healthy snacks like vegetables.**
- **Drink lots of water each day.**

Food Addiction Pattern (Page 1)

There is a distinct pattern that one experiences in one's addiction to food. This pattern revolves around the search for the object of one's desire. This object is often something sweet, sugary, salty, or processed. A food addiction pattern looks something like this:

- Searches for a "hit" on foods that will satisfy the addiction.
- Experiences an intense compulsion and/or desire for the food.
- Has a strong, all-encompassing focus on getting that food.
- Eats and often overeats.
- Experiences withdrawal symptoms when the food is taken away.
- As tolerance develops over time, stronger cravings also develop.

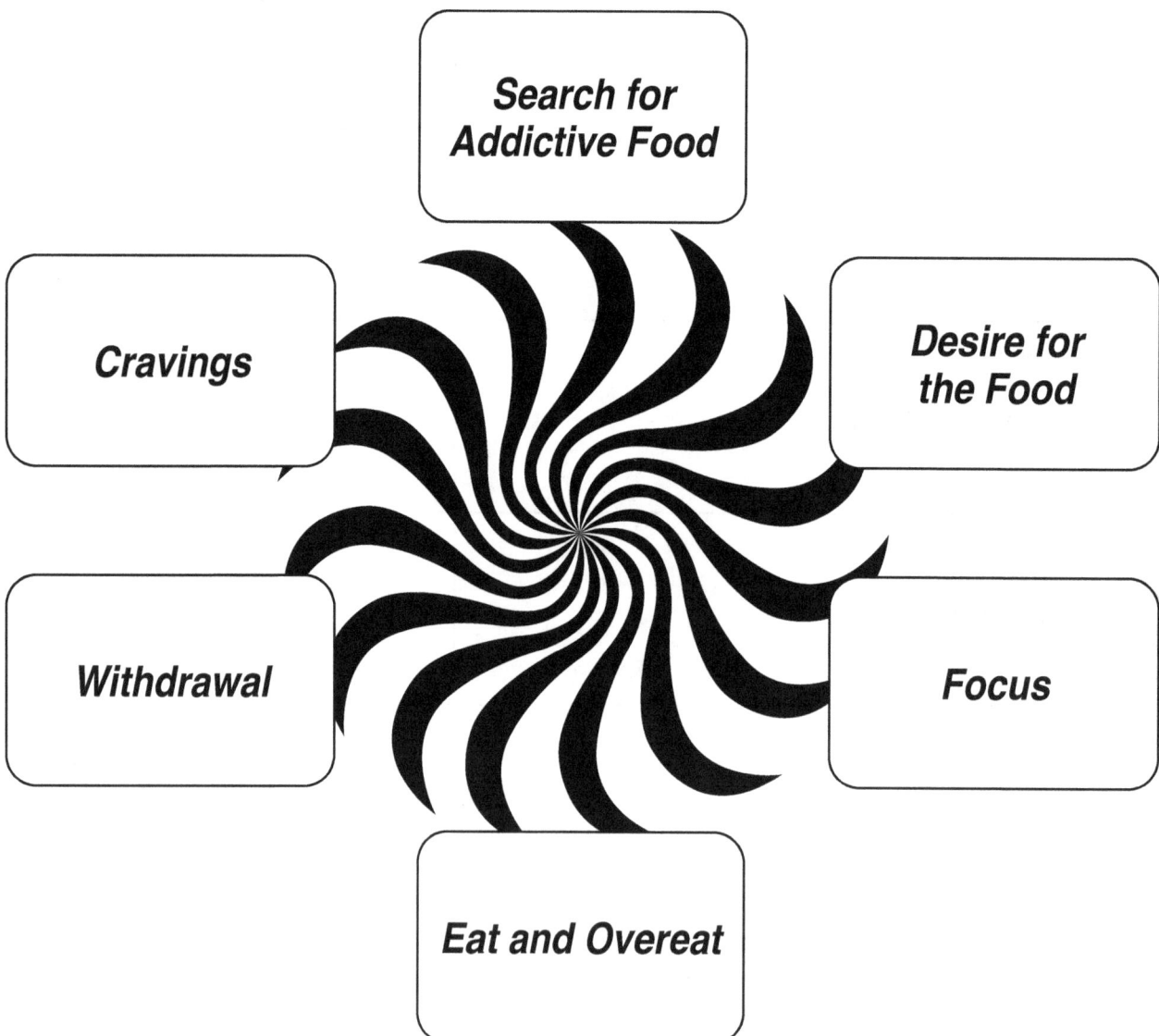

Search for Addictive Food

Cravings

Desire for the Food

Withdrawal

Focus

Eat and Overeat

(Continued on the next page.)

Food Addiction Pattern (Page 2)

There is a distinct pattern that you experience in your addiction to food. This pattern revolves around your search for the object of your desire.

Next to each box, write about how you keep the food addiction cycle alive through these six behaviors:

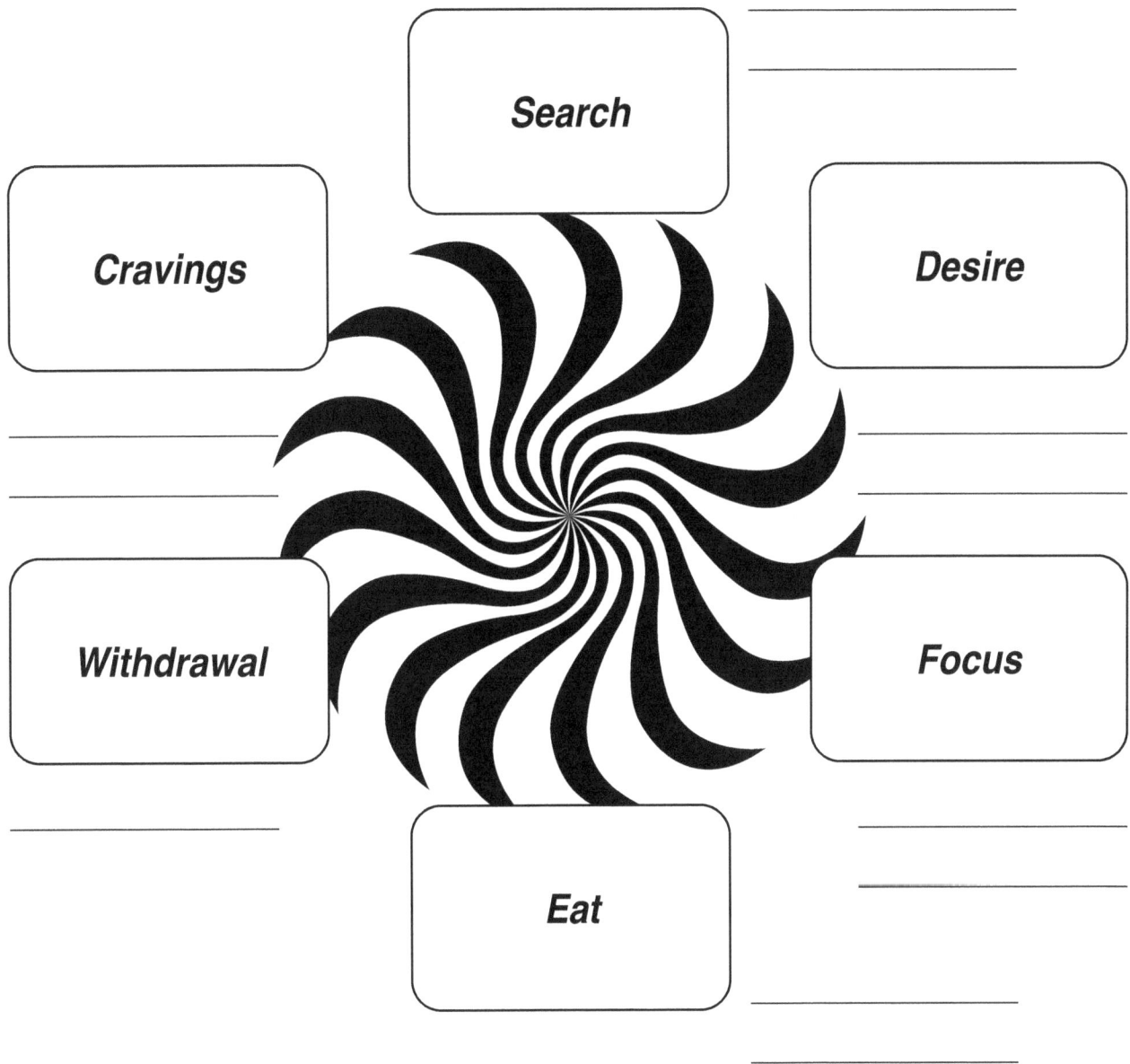

Search

Cravings

Desire

Withdrawal

Focus

Eat

TIP: Allow time for your taste buds to change and your cravings to diminish. Once you switch your diet to healthy foods, you will crave less sugary and processed foods.

Don't give up! It takes time for your tastes to change.

Healthful Suggestions

Recovering from a food addiction requires a lifestyle change that is often a lifelong commitment. It can take time to become rebalanced through healthy nutrition.

The suggestions below are important steps in the healing process. Write about your experience with them.

Use portion sizes to your advantage. Eat small portions of desserts and treats.

_____
_____
_____

Strive for variety and balance when eating a meal. Try to create meals full of interesting flavors and textures with lots of variety in food groups so you don't crave snacks afterwards.

_____
_____
_____

Plan ahead to make sure healthy foods are readily available and other "junk" foods are less available.

_____
_____
_____

Eat in moderation rather than overeating.

_____
_____
_____

Completely cut sugar and artificial sweeteners out of your diet. Once you stop eating them, the cravings will slowly go away.

_____
_____
_____

Be aware of fat-free and low-fat foods. Food manufacturers take the fat out of their products but they replace it with sweeteners and artificial ingredients (which are usually not healthy!) to compensate for the missing flavor.

_____
_____
_____

Choose two tips to implement this week. Write about how that will look.

_____
_____
_____

Quotes about Healthy Routines

On the lines that follow the four quotes below, describe which quote(s) speak to you and your healthy routines.

I exercise, and I eat reasonably, and I don't want to look at myself being out of shape. That would depress me.
~ Judy Sheindlin

Each night, when I go to sleep, I die. And the next morning, when I wake up, I am reborn.
~ Mahatma Gandhi

To keep the body in good health is a duty...otherwise we shall not be able to keep our mind strong and clear.
~ Buddha

All the money in the world can't buy you back good health.
~ Reba McEntire

Which quote especially speaks to you about healthy routines? Why?

_____

_____

_____

_____

_____

_____

_____

_____

_____

_____

Food

Coping Strategies

Name _____

Date _____

Food Addiction Symptoms Assessment
Introduction and Directions

People who are addicted to food demonstrate many symptoms. They have a distinct relationship with food, get cravings for certain foods, get frustrated if their cravings are not satisfied, and often overeat.

This assessment contains 20 statements designed to help you explore your symptoms of a food addiction. Read each of the statements and decide whether the statement describes you or not. If the statement does describe you, circle the number in the YES column next to that item. If the statement does not describe you, circle the number in the NO column next to that item.

In the following example, the circled 2 indicates that the statement does describe the person completing the inventory:

	YES	NO

In thinking about my eating habits ...

I am preoccupied with food . . . . (2) 1

This is not a test. Since there are no right or wrong answers, do not spend too much time thinking about your answers. Be sure to respond to every statement.

BE HONEST!

If you choose, no one else needs to see the results.

(Turn to the next page and begin.)

Food Addiction Symptoms Assessment

Name _____ Date _____

**This will only be accurate if you respond honestly.
No one else needs to see this if you choose to keep it private.**

	YES	NO

In thinking about my eating habits ...

	YES	NO
I am preoccupied with food.	2	1
I often binge eat.	2	1
I lose control over how much I eat.	2	1
I experience a negative impact on my family life.	2	1
I lack social interaction.	2	1
I spend a lot of money on fast foods.	2	1
I eat compulsively.	2	1
I have tried to stop overeating but I always relapse.	2	1
I feel the need to eat food for emotional release.	2	1
I eat alone to avoid attention.	2	1
I often eat until I experience physical discomfort or pain.	2	1
I have frequent cravings for certain foods.	2	1
I crave food even after I have finished a meal.	2	1
I often eat much more than I intended.	2	1
I feel guilty after eating particular foods.	2	1
I make excuses about why food craving is okay.	2	1
I hide my consumption of unhealthy foods from others.	2	1
I cannot control my craving or eating unhealthy foods.	2	1
I eat even though I know the amount of food can cause me harm.	2	1
I worry about premature death.	2	1

TOTAL = _____

*Go to the next page for scoring assessment results,
profile interpretation, and assessment description.*

Food Addiction Symptoms Assessment

Descriptions and Profile Interpretations

The assessment you just completed is designed to measure the symptoms of a food addiction.

Count the scores you circled on the assessment. Put that number on the assessment line marked TOTAL. Using that number, place an X on the line representing your score.

20 = Low	30 = Moderate	40 = High

Assessment Profile Interpretation

Even one YES item on the scale can suggest that you are exhibiting symptoms of an addiction to food. The HIGHER your score on the Food Addiction Symptoms Assessment, the greater effect your eating and your relationship with food is having on you and your entire life.

What surprises you about your score?

_____

_____

_____

Who is a trusted person you can share the assessment with, who can help you with your food addiction? Use name codes.

_____

_____

_____

Go back to the assessment and highlight the items for which you circled YES.
Keep the page as a reminder of things you need to work on in order to
discontinue your food addiction and have the ability to lead a full, healthy life.

Out of Sight, Out of Mind

When people have a food addiction, they tend to eat anything and everything that is available, especially when they have a craving. With food, the old adage "out of sight out of mind" often applies. If you can see something in your kitchen, you are apt to eat it when you get a craving. Buying less of the food you're trying to limit is key to a moderate approach. For example, you may want to limit your purchase of processed food, sugary soda, and sweets. Rather, you could stock your kitchen with healthy snack foods and desserts like dark chocolate, nuts, vegetables, berries, fruit, and yogurt.

In the spaces that follow, identify some of the food and drinks you need to buy less of, and some things you need to buy more of.

Food/Drinks I Need to Buy Less Frequently

Food/Drinks I Need to Buy More Frequently

Successful weight loss takes programming, not willpower.
~ Phil McGraw

Set Goals

People addicted to food often lack goals. What goals have you set for overcoming your addiction to food?

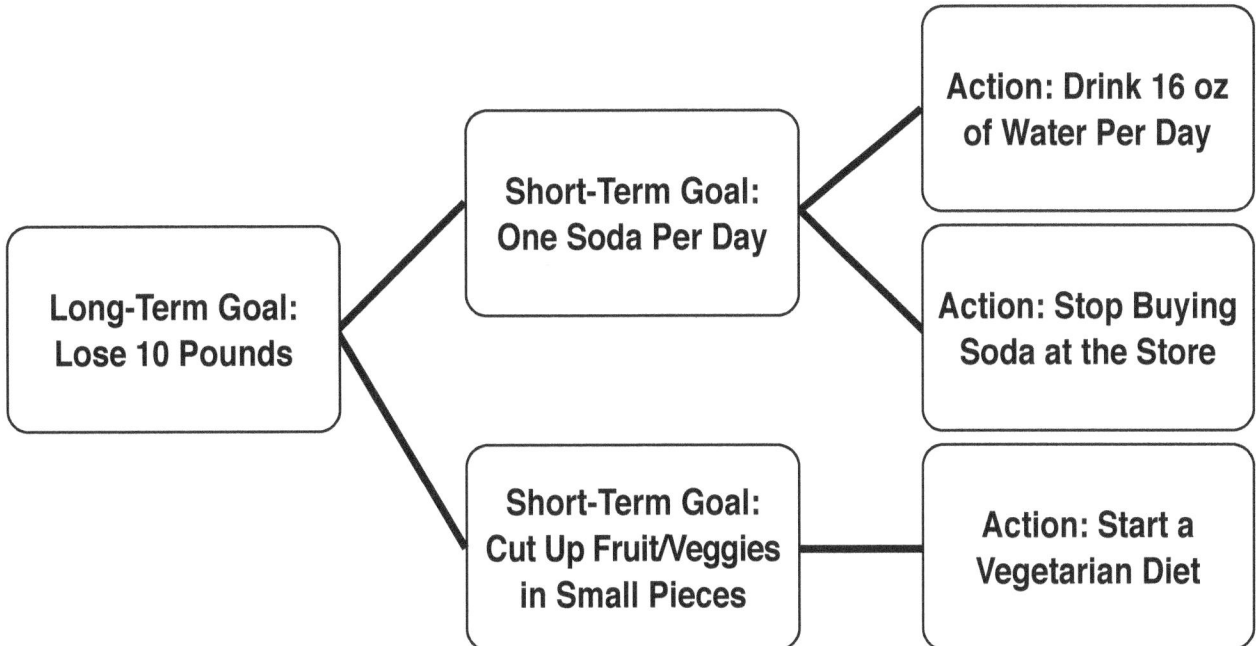

```
                                                    ┌──────────────────┐
                                                    │ Action: Drink 16 oz │
                                                    │ of Water Per Day    │
                                                    └──────────────────┘
                          ┌──────────────────┐
                          │ Short-Term Goal: │
                          │ One Soda Per Day │
                          └──────────────────┘
                                                    ┌──────────────────┐
┌──────────────────┐                                │ Action: Stop Buying │
│ Long-Term Goal:  │                                │ Soda at the Store   │
│ Lose 10 Pounds   │                                └──────────────────┘
└──────────────────┘
                          ┌──────────────────────┐
                          │ Short-Term Goal:     │  ┌──────────────────┐
                          │ Cut Up Fruit/Veggies │  │ Action: Start a  │
                          │ in Small Pieces      │  │ Vegetarian Diet  │
                          └──────────────────────┘  └──────────────────┘
```

Now you do it: 1 Long-Term Goal, 2 Short-Term Goals, and 3 Actions you will take.

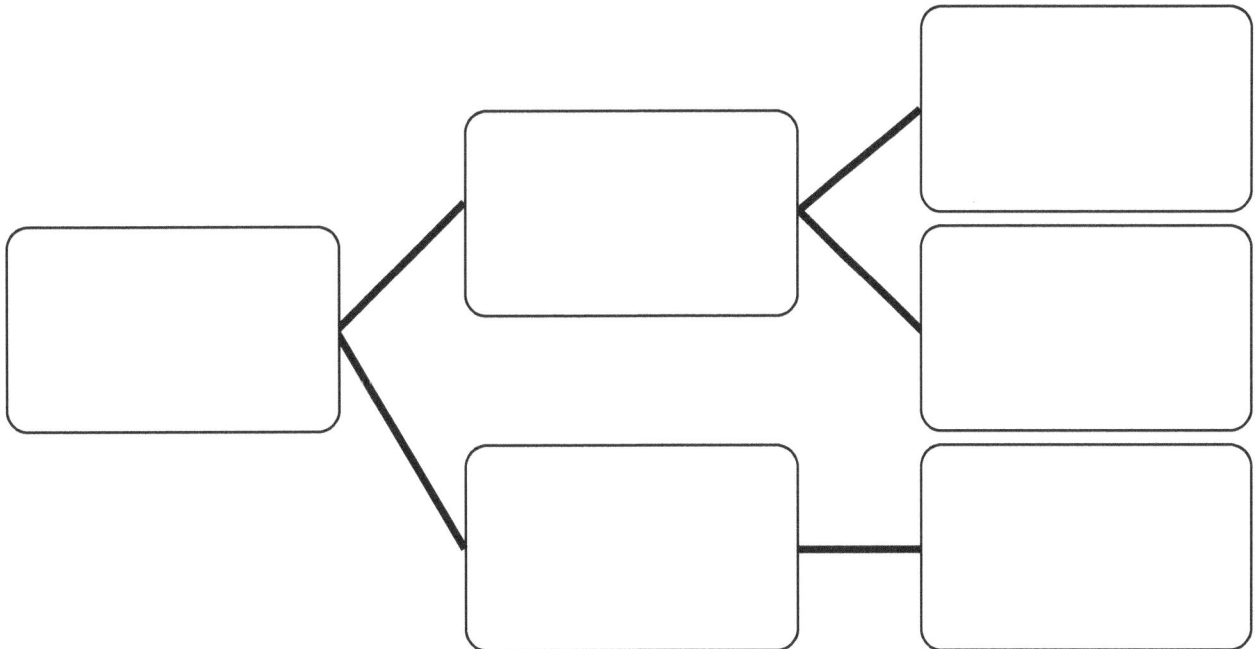

```
                                                    ┌──────────────────┐
                                                    │                  │
                          ┌──────────────────┐      │                  │
                          │                  │      └──────────────────┘
                          │                  │
                          │                  │      ┌──────────────────┐
┌──────────────────┐      └──────────────────┘      │                  │
│                  │                                 │                  │
│                  │                                 └──────────────────┘
│                  │      ┌──────────────────┐
└──────────────────┘      │                  │      ┌──────────────────┐
                          │                  │      │                  │
                          │                  │      │                  │
                          └──────────────────┘      └──────────────────┘
```

Use this formula to set multiple goals and actions to overcome your food addiction. FYI: when people cut up fruit and veggies in small, attractive ways, they are more likely to eat more of them.

How Do You See You?

What do you see when you look in the mirror? Oftentimes what you see is what others project onto you. For example, if your partner makes subtle jokes about your weight, it can affect your self-image. If your parent tells you that your clothes are too tight, you realize that it is obvious that you gained weight.

PRETEND THERE ARE TWO "MIRRORS" BELOW

Column #1: Pretend you are looking in the "How I Think Others See Me" mirror and draw a picture or a collage of words that describe how you think others see you.

Column #2: Now move onto the "How I Actually See Myself" mirror on the right and draw a picture or a collage of words that describe how you see yourself.

How I Think Others See Me	How I Actually See Myself

Which of the two mirrors is more accurate? Explain why. _____

_____

_____

Overall Well-Being

A food addiction is often a culmination of many different factors that interact.

Below, identify how your lifestyle and eating behavior is contributing to your food addiction, which is affecting your overall well-being, and how you can do better.

Lifestyle Factors	My Eating Behavior	How It Affects My Overall Well-Being	How I Can Do Better
Example: Food choices	*I eat a bag of potato chips daily.*	*I have high blood pressure from the salt and then I gain weight.*	*I could eat carrot sticks instead.*
Food Choices			
Exercise			
Sleep			
Relaxation			
Support System			
Spiritual Wellness			
Other			
Other			

You can add five years to your lifespan by just making intelligent lifestyle choices.
~ Lamman Rucker

Unhealthy Comparisons

Making comparisons with other people in their life, or celebrities on TV or the movies, can encourage people to lose weight in any way they possibly can, just so they can look like those people. This can turn into an <u>eating disorder</u> (an illness that people experience with their eating behaviors and related thoughts and emotions). People with eating disorders typically become preoccupied with food and their body image.

Identify the people to whom you compare yourself in relation to your body image.

The Person I Compare Myself to (Name Code)	How I Know or Have Seen This Person	How I Compare Myself	Is My Comparison Reasonable? Why or Why Not
Example: SAA	She's an actress and stays slim all the time in every movie.	I want to look like her.	Maybe not reasonable. She probably has people taking care of her, feeding her the right food, and making sure she wears slimming clothes.

Where are most of your comparisons made (in person, on social media, movies, etc.)?

_____

What can you say to yourself when you are comparing?

_____

The Danger of Comparing

Below are some tips related to the danger of comparing yourself to others, and some prompts for you to journal your thoughts and feelings.

Read each of the statements and journal your responses on the lines below.

Become aware of when you are comparing yourself to others. Are you in the mall, reading a magazine, surfing the internet, or on social media sites?

_____

_____

_____

Celebrate yourself rather than tearing yourself down. How can you celebrate yourself more?

_____

_____

_____

How do you tear yourself down?

_____

_____

_____

Limit your time admiring celebrities. They are people with many of the same issues as you! How much time do you spend looking online or reading magazines looking at celebrities? To whom do you compare yourself most?

_____

_____

_____

Be aware of the negative thoughts and feelings that accompany your comparisons with others. What thoughts usually go through your head and what feelings accompany these thoughts?

_____

_____

_____

Focus on your own positive features. What are your most positive features (personality, traits, characteristics, interests, etc.)?

_____

_____

_____

Who or What Is Holding You Back?

Who is holding you back from breaking free of your food addiction?

What Is Holding Me Back?	How This Occurs	What I Can Do to Change the Dynamics
Example: My partner buys junk food and I keep eating it.	*If it's around, I eat it. I try telling him but he says, "Don't eat it."*	*I will ask my partner to put his snacks in a less visible place and practice making better choices by not eating it.*

What is holding you back from breaking free of your food addiction?

What Is Holding Me Back?	How This Occurs	What I Can Do to Change the Dynamics
Example: I work in an office where there is junk food everywhere!	*I go into a meeting and everyone is munching.*	*I can bring my own healthy snacks.*

© 2022 WHOLE PERSON ASSOCIATES, 101 WEST 2ND STREET, SUITE 203, DULUTH MN 55802 • 800-247-6789 • WHOLEPERSON.COM

Thoughts, Feelings, and Actions

It's important to understand the unique connection between your thoughts, feelings, and actions. Believe it or not, they drive each other in producing your eating behaviors. What thoughts and emotions do you associate with food and eating?

Complete the table that follows. You can have multiple answers in each column.

Thoughts	Feelings	Actions
Example: I know that I am going to have many physical problems because of the unhealthy way that I eat.	*I feel sad and frustrated most of the time, even when I am eating junk food!*	*I want to start cutting down on sweets, so I started substituting a small piece of dark chocolate for cake. Then the next day I ate three pieces of cake.*

Relapse Prevention

It is important to identify the feelings, places, people, and foods that will trigger a relapse in your eating behavior. Plan for what you will do when you get a craving, or when a friend brings over homemade cookies. You may have to change your routine by avoiding certain situations, or by driving further to avoid going by the bakery that you stop at every day, or by explaining to people you no longer eat sweets.

Below, create a plan for the feelings, places, people, and foods that trigger a relapse.

My Triggers	How I Am Affected	My Plan to Prevent Relapse
Feelings		
Places		
People		
Foods		

When you relapse, what are the foods you usually give in to?

_____

_____

How can you avoid those particular foods?

_____

_____

Social Pressure

Social Pressure is the direct influence on people by another person or group.

What are the social pressures, put onto you by people or groups in your life that influence your eating habits? Do you feel obligated to eat at social gatherings and meetings involving food, where there is little choice about what to eat and/or drink?

Identify your social pressure situations in the squares below:

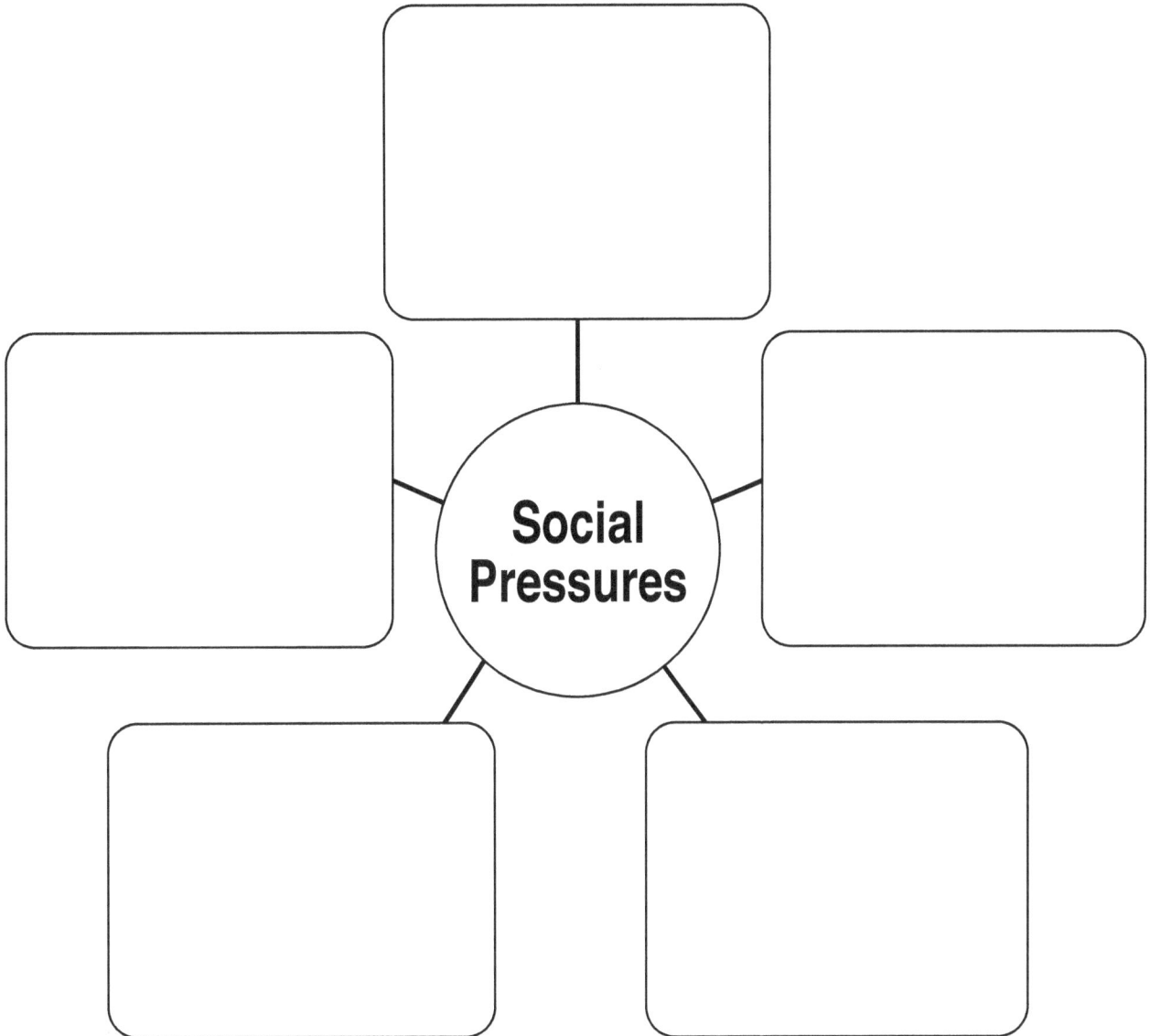

Social Pressures

What can you do to minimize the negative effects of social pressure?
- Tell others that you are a vegetarian and hold out for veggies.
- Let people know you want to eat in healthy ways.
- Eat something healthy beforehand.
- Assertively say "no thank you!"
- Bring your own food.

You Are Not Your Food Addictions

For people addicted to food, their entire existence is usually wrapped up in what they want to eat, when they are going to eat, where they will eat, where the snacks will be, and how they can give into their cravings immediately. One way to break this cycle is to focus on expanding other aspects of your life that have meaning.

You are not defined by your addiction and you are much more than your addiction.

In each of the boxes below, write, draw, or doodle four aspects of your life that have nothing to do with food, and are meaningful to you, which you would like to expand. Describe how you will enrich these areas. (Classes, research, hobby, read, sport, choir, etc.)

I will enrich the above by _____ _____

I will enrich the above by _____ _____

I will enrich the above by _____ _____

I will enrich the above by _____ _____

Stimulation of Unhealthy Eating Tendencies

If you are addicted to certain foods or certain ways of eating, you probably find that specific environments or situations stimulate unhealthy eating tendencies. For example, when watching TV, you need a snack; when you look at social media you see ads for foods; when you are reading magazines that show people with perfect bodies, you are affected by your need to have a perfect body but can't because of food!

Below, explore the environments and situations that stimulate your unhealthy eating.

Environment or Situation	What Occurs	How I Could Avoid This Environment or Situation
Example: *Watching television*	*I see advertisements between programs, and I crave snacks.*	*Keep a healthy snack available.*
Watching television		
Reading a magazine		
Walking by a food vendor on the street		
Invited to someone's house for dinner		
Shopping at grocery store		
Cooking dinner for other people		

How can you better sustain eating less food?

_____

_____

_____

"I resolve to eat less food" sounds good in theory, but it's often hard to sustain. And if you believe that it's all willpower, then you're likely to be upset with yourself if you don't succeed.
~ Dean Ornish

Look to Food for a Way Out

Read the quote that follows, then answer the questions that follow it.

I realized that I couldn't knowingly look to food for a way out when it
had so clearly led me here. It wasn't hunger that beckoned me to eat more.
It wasn't my stomach that needed to be reconciled. It was shame.
It was guilt. And food can't remedy such things.
~ Andie Mitchell

What does the above quote mean to you?

_____
_____
_____

How have your eating habits led you to where you are currently?

_____
_____
_____

If it wasn't hunger that beckoned you to eat more, what did?

_____
_____
_____

Of what are you ashamed? Describe ways you can overcome your shame without eating.

_____
_____
_____

About what do you feel guilty? Describe ways you can overcome your guilt without eating.

_____
_____
_____

Food Addiction Coping Strategies

People who are addicted to food need different strategies for coping with craving, triggers, and situations in which food is present. Below are strategies that can help you in managing your eating behavior.

Be Kind to Yourself

Managing a food addiction is a challenging task. You need to be kind to yourself during this process. If you relapse and eat something you know you shouldn't, pick yourself up and start again by setting modest, manageable goals.

What do you typically do when you relapse?

_____

_____

_____

How does that hurt you in the long term?

_____

_____

Avoid Self-Criticism

Avoid focusing on relapses and self-criticism. This type of thinking will only prompt you to eat more.

How do you criticize yourself if you relapse?

_____

_____

_____

_____

Reward Yourself

Acknowledge ANY progress you make with non-food-related rewards that you enjoy.

For example, you could treat yourself to a massage after a week of regular exercise or go camping after a month of healthier eating. How can you reward yourself?

_____

_____

_____

_____

_____

My Supporters

Don't be afraid to rely on trusted others, including friends, family members, members of the community, and professionals for help in overcoming your addiction to food. You will find that various members of your support network can support and provide you with different ways of improving your eating behavior. Making a change in your eating habits is difficult, but it is attainable with support.

Create a list of those trusted people who can help you and describe how they can support you.

Types of Supporters	Name Codes of Trusted People	Their Home Phone, Cell Phone, Text Info, or Email Address	How Can They Support Me
Friends			
Family Members			
Members of the Community			
Medical Professionals			
Other			
Other			

© 2022 WHOLE PERSON ASSOCIATES, 101 WEST 2ND STREET, SUITE 203, DULUTH MN 55802 • 800-247-6789 • WHOLEPERSON.COM

Quotes about Coping with a Food Addiction

On the lines that follow the quotes, describe what one of these quotes means to you and how it applies to YOUR life.

Withdrawal occurs once a person stops eating any addictive food. Though abstaining from foods is a contentious subject in the scientific literature, there is no question that it will cause a level of discomfort that often drives addicts back to eating.
~ Vera Tarman

You must have the willpower to avoid what is bad. It's simple: If you indulge, you will develop a bulge.
~ Jeetendra

If you tell me I can't eat something, I'll obsess over it and end up overeating!
~ Octavia Spencer

While overeating would be seen by some as an indulgence of self, it is in fact a profound rejection of self. It is a moment of self-betrayal and self-punishment, and anything but a commitment to one's own well-being.
~ Marianne Williamson

Which of the quotes speaks to you and your food addiction?

_____

_____

_____

_____

_____

_____

_____

_____

_____

_____

WholePerson

Whole Person Associates is the leading publisher of training resources for professionals who empower people to create and maintain healthy lifestyles. Our creative resources will help you work effectively with your clients in the areas of stress management, wellness promotion, mental health, and life skills.

Please visit us at our website: **WholePerson.com**. You can check out our entire line of products, place an order, request our print catalog, and sign up for our monthly special notifications.

Whole Person Associates
800-247-6789
Books@WholePerson.com